The Promised Human Destiny

Reflections of W. Deen Mohammed

Edited by Ronald B. Shaheed

The Promised Human Destiny

Reflections of W. Deen Mohammed

Heartfelt thanks to Imam Nasir Ahmad for his tireless effort in transcribing the audio digital material from Imam W. Deen Mohammed used to compile this book. May Allah grant Imam W. Deen Mohammed the highest level of His Paradise.

Edited and Published by Imam Ronald B. Shaheed

2014

ISBN 978-0-692-23618-5

CONTENTS

FOREWORD

Imam W. Deen Mohammed was one of the most influential religious leaders of these modern times. A celebrated scholar of religion, Dr. C. Eric Lincoln, said of him:

"Wallace Deen Muhammed is a dreamer, but he is a dreamer-cum-realist, and gentle, sensitive, and self-effacing. History may yet prove him to be one of the most astute religious leaders of this age, regardless of communion. A lifelong student of Islam, fluent in Arabic, and well conversant with the nuances of Qur'anic ideology and its institutionalized projections, Wallace is no less a keen and perceptive observer of the American scene. Therein lies his potential for achievement and service to Islam." C. Eric Lincoln, "The Muslim Mission in the Context of American Social History", *African-American Religion: Interpretive Essays in History and Culture*, T. E. Fulop & A. J. Raboteau, Routledge, New York, NY, 1997, p. 288

His lifestyle was that of the common neighbor and citizen that one can find in any community in the United States. He did not favor bringing attention to himself and yet what he thought, what he said and did had a profound effect on and garnered respect from governmental leaders, religious and educational leaders, institutions and individuals from across the world. He was the leader of the largest indigenous Islamic community in the Western hemisphere from 1975 until his passing in 2008.

This is a continuing work which follows, *Thoughts for Searchers Seeking to Understand Life,* one of the initial attempts to compile, organize and present to the world Imam W. Deen Mohammed's intimate thoughts and reflections. On September 19, 2007 in the comfortable surroundings of his modest home in Markham, Illinois, he said:

"Okay, so I have told you all about the burden that I have on my heart and any way you can help, help. What you record of me I feel good about it because I don't want everything to die with me and be lost. And what I share with you all I'll give it to you in writing, that it's you all's responsibility. You have no obligation to anybody, my office,

the Ministry, The Mosque Cares, or anything. (If you want to appeal to the people to finance putting some of it in writing or all of it writing for the future, you can do that with my support. But you have no obligation to give the responsibility to anybody and that includes the money. If you get money for it use it for yourself. If you want to give a donation from it, that's up to you all. I'm serious! This is not something I'm just thinking about. I looked at it a long time ago. Yes, this is a project for you all. You don't owe anybody anything; not me, nobody anything. It's a service. It's valuable. This is my way and I believe G_d is moving me to do this. This is my way of putting it into your charge. And don't think that some of this doesn't have a place on the bookshelves or libraries of higher institutions of knowledge, higher institutions of learning.

So I leave it to you all to put it in form; put it in form and on paper. As you look at what I've said, if you look at it, put it all on paper and then look at it and say, "Well, he's talking on this idea, or such and such an idea in this focus, at this particular time. And at several other times when we met with him he came back to this idea. Maybe his focus changed, maybe it didn't." So, you have to look at that and when you look at it and you put it together you're probably going to see a progression. Once you see a progression, then begin typing. Set your sight on that because there should be a progression. For any discussion of an idea there should be a progression and when you find that progression, then collect everything that shows the progression...So, you think about it and maybe you'll come with some other language, or language that would identify the whole of it, like a title of it. I am slow to give a title, but just a caption or language that would hold it all together, or would identify it as a piece of literature or a discussion of serious matters for understanding life as people of G_d, as people in religion. Believe me, there are people who are up, up, up, who'll really appreciate it. They don't live on earth. They live in the sky."

One of Imam W. Deen Mohammed's preferred topics for discussion and reflection was the destiny of man, or the human being. In an intimate conversation at his home he once shared that he believed nothing happened to him in his life by accident. He believed that there was a wonderful destiny, established by

G_d, for the individual person. But, more importantly, he believed G_d promises a wonderful destiny for the human community at large; that one day the world will come to see itself as one community under G_d.

Five prophets, or human types, stand out in Imam Mohammed's reflections on the destiny of humanity at large and they each represent a progression towards the destiny established by G_d when He created the first human person. Consequently, Imam W. Deen Mohammed's reflection on each one of these prophets has suggested the title for each chapter of this publication, beginning with Adam and ending with Muhammed.

I pray that in my compiling and editing these thoughts and reflections of Imam W. Deen Mohammed on the destiny of mankind I have achieved some degree of success.

The Editor

Introduction

Destiny is in finding how to establish one's self support. The soul needs to find its support and this support, once found, gives every individual that experiences it spiritual self-support. The process is initiated or set into motion by human life's universal soul. That is to say that though we have individual souls, we all have one common soul and that is the soul of all people, all human beings, the universal human soul.

The soul's life force is always reaching out, or reaching for wholeness that is understanding; understanding that makes our life acceptable and comfortable in a situation with other people and other nations. After finding common existence and common spirit, a cosmological finding as I see it and as I believe it's revealed in scripture, the scripture we call the Abrahamic scriptures, we can reason our way or our path to self-identity and purpose.

Islam first addresses purpose, the purpose for human life and the purpose for human life in Islam is to serve the Creator, Whose common name and proper name for Muslims is Allah. The human soul engages a process for locating its security and discovers its existence is placed, firstly, in cosmology, the study of the universe. The soul's life force is now liberated. After finding its first place it is liberated to establish self-support and secure its viable self-interest.

Self-interest can be selfishness. But, if it takes this route from the universe or from the cosmos and seeks its destiny from the cosmos to its place where it is going to reside and have its life, it will not be selfish. Connecting cosmologically, an environment framework is now reached for identifying our soul's inclusiveness. From this cosmological home a direction is found mapping frameworks that will support one's human existence, beginning in cosmic wholeness, thereafter, in planetary or global wholeness; further inward to frameworks for the national and social interest and security.

Destinies are natural homes for the soul

Our soul seeks the security that is natural for it. Some of us are secured in situations that will not rest our soul because those situations are not natural. Destinies are natural homes for our souls. Destiny is home. Returning from cosmology, the human soul arrives at its address in its national boundary to view itself as a member in its cosmological, global, national and social family. Self-support is support of family. Families supporting themselves and contributing to the support of others have found home for the soul and can realize then a true sense of security.

We thank Allah, that is, G_d, Who made all that is in existence and made it for us to mate our intelligence with that universe, or with that creation, so that our life will develop intelligently and we will have a condition that is a must for us now in this time of global reality and global inclusion. Allah says in Arabic, "Wabtagi feemaa aataa kal laahud daaral aakhirata wa laa tansa nasibaka minad dunya. Seek with what G_d has given you as a means to work with, the home in the future or the home at the end. But don't neglect your share in this world". The word, "Akhira", literally means, "End, the latter". If you are going in a direction the end of it is "Akhira". He says, "Seek the home of the end, the destination, the destiny set by G_d, not your destiny set by you. Seek the home in that destiny. When you have evolved as I will and plan that you evolve, that will be the end. That will be the last of it. The last of it will be when you arrive at the complete life that I am evolving you upon. When you arrive at that complete life that will be the last". Doesn't that make sense?

Evolution is trying to fulfill something. It is trying to complete something. It wants to complete something that is in the human life or in the life. It wants to complete the pattern that is in the life and establish the life upon its complete pattern. That is evolution and that is religion in the proper sense in the Qur'an. G_d says seek that and what else does He say about it? Surely that life that is promised in the end is better than this life in value and also in quantity; not just in value. Do you think we have a lot now? When that time comes we will have much more. Do you think we have achieved civil society? When that time comes it will be even more beautiful and more correct, more just, more virtuous, etc. than it is now. G_d evolves us for the life of excellence and value but also for comforts. The promise of the life after is all about comforts, too. He is going to give you amply and give even more than what your needs are. This is the promise. He is going to give you abundantly. It will be a life in every good sense. He says that of life its promise is better than the life of this world. It is better in terms of value and also in quantity.

He says, "Don't forget or neglect your share of the world", why? It is because you have been led by pious people who claim divinity, who claim righteousness, who claim purity, to believe that the material world corrupts your soul and you shouldn't attach yourself to it. You should not want to develop it. Leave it to others. These developers who develop towns and cities, do you think they come from the holy rollers? They don't come from them, nor the rabbis, the shieks that do dhikrs until they fall asleep on their beads, etc. These are people who go to the extremes of the spiritual life and neglect the flesh and the material interest and feed on it, though all the money you make they won't turn it down.

The well balanced community

The community is called, "Ummatul wustaa", in the Qur'an and it means, "The well-balanced community". It is not going to the extreme of spirituality and it's not going to the extreme of materialism. It keeps the mean, the balance, so that the people are not oppressed by materialism and not oppressed by spiritualism, because both can oppress us.

When we are told over and over again to believe in the, "Akhirah", the purpose is to keep us futuristic, looking ahead to the future, always. "Akhirah", means the last part, the latter and this, "dunya" is what? We are to live a life of uprightness and benefit from the, "ulaa", that means the dunya. But the dunya has reference to the material world and "ulaa" means all of it, the life that you establish for yourself by making use of the material world, your relationship to the things that are natural, the resources, etc.; and your relationship to the things that you have produced, man made things.

So you have a relationship with that and then you form certain sentiments and you become emotionally attached, sentimentally attached to these things. You then form relationships with each other. You come together and you love each other because you like money. You have a whole family just living to make money. Now, even your relationship with one another or with each other has been influenced by the dunya. All of that is, "al ulaa". It is all the attachments that you have to the material things; the way you see each other and value each other, because it is affected by the material things and not by the hope of the true believers; the hope in the day of righteousness and justice, fairness and comforts without corruption.

Material world gives man ideas for forming religion

When you look at dunya and deen (religion) they have similar letters. So really the material world has given man his ideas for forming his religion and I could quickly relate it to you in comparative religion. There are rain gods. Rain comes from this dunya. There are river gods. River is dunya. There are mountain gods, lightning gods, thunder gods, fertility gods and they are dunya.

They believed that their land was so fertile that they thought a god was behind it. Man was made to be thankful, so if he comes into all of these things he wants to find Who or What is responsible for this. "I owe whatever is responsible for this. I didn't make it. I owe it thanks". So he forms his own idea of G_d from his relationship with the dunya. He likes it and it works well for him. He starts preaching it, giving it to his family and others. Most of the path of evolution to come into the proper religion or spiritual life in the best sense for humans on this earth, most of that path of growth, progress and evolution, was a path where man was engaging the material world and coming up with ideas, even his religious ideas. In fact, he came up with religious ideas before he came up with scientific understanding.

There was a teacher and imam that I respected a whole lot. He died not long ago, may he be in Paradise. We were just socializing because we never had any real classes, except he taught me Urdu and recitation of Qur'an until he heard my recitation. Then he said, "Yours is better than mine" and that was because mine came from a man who spoke pure Arabic and his came from Indians who did not speak pure Arabic. He said to me, "Our kalimah, the creed, begins with a negative, not a positive". It begins with, "Laa, no". Isn't that the way man has progressed, by saying, "No", to things that did not respect his intelligence? Abraham said, "No", all night long and when the sun rose up in the morning he said, "No", for the last time. He came to the conclusion that the Cause behind those things was G_d, not those things themselves. So he had to say, "Laa", a lot. That is what man was saying all along the long road of his progress on the path of evolution. He was saying, "No", to stones, to lightning and he finally said, "Yes", to the Cause behind all of it, the Unseen.

A new perception of reality

Some of you might say, "Akhirah", is the life after death and that is true. But it's the death of what? It is the death of your thinking on the wrong path. You die to that thinking that keeps leading you wrong and you come alive to a new thinking, a new perception of reality. Then, you have life after this life, or life after death. "Well, what about the funeral service? What about that person who is put in the ground and they're gone? We hope they left some good sons behind them to pray for their souls. Is there any hope for them?" Their best hope is their good name that they left behind them with us and their good hopes that we hope we will not lose or violate. Isn't that the prayer of the janazah? What we valued in them is their good name and good works they left with us and their good children that they left behind that will pray for their souls.

A new earth and a new heaven

Never should we give up hope that there is a chance for a person who dies a death like that and never think that is the big important matter that is addressed in scripture. It is not addressing this attachment to the mortal life and wanting to be in this flesh, again. Scripture is talking about the life to come when the perception changes and you stop seeing this world as you saw it before; when you see it as communication, ayats (signs) from G_d and you start to read G_d's will and His plan in these material things. That is a new kingdom, a new earth and a new heaven. We will come into a new heaven, a new earth and a new life; one that will not perish but will be eternal. One might say, "You can't take that with you, can you?" I can take that with me to the grave and smile before death. I can look death in the face and I'll be smiling until the last breath is gone from my body, because I have certainly been freed.

Falsehood was ever doomed to perish

I don't know what he had in mind but I can say as Dr. King said, "I've been to the mountain top" and go out, peacefully, knowing that G_d has set man on a course and no matter how troublesome, how horrible, how dark and uncertain man's life becomes in his world, G_d has set man upon a course and it is going to continue. Nothing can stop it. It is truly inevitable and nothing can stop it. Nothing can keep it from coming about. One day all of man's guess work will be pushed aside and not accepted in religion and only the truth will be established or accepted. We are coming very close to a time like that right now. Many are looking at the world, the streets, at things happening in small places, but I know what's happening in big places and they are working with faith and confidence that this world is going to be filled with truth and falsehood is going to perish. "Now the truth has come and falsehood perishes. It was ever doomed to perish" (Qur'an). Even when we thought it was everlasting G_d is saying, "No, it has the nature, it already has the cancers in it to kill it. It is doomed to perish." It is born with a cancer, terminal disease and G_d said it is ever doomed to perish.

Our life in the future

So, when we say, "Al-Akhirah", we should understand that Muslims live for the future. G_d promises us a future. That's what we live for and that's in the final stage of this great plan that G_d put us upon when He created us a part of this world, this creation. And we will be approaching the final stage in that plan. We are already there. We will be seeing it unfold and that will be the Hereafter. Allah says (in Qur'an), "When they see that they will say, 'This resembles what we had before'." You might ask, "What about our loved ones? Will we be reconnected, rejoined?" It says, "Yes, you shall be rejoined there with your loved ones; that is, if your loved ones earn it, too".

What about us who are here whose souls G_d has brought to completion and we are ready for the Hereafter? Five hundred or ten thousand years from now, if our flesh descendants or anybody who reconnects or ties themselves into our life, discovers it and they connect themselves back to our life and hear what we did, how we thought and lived, don't you know we will be living in the future with them? That is a bigger hope than wanting this old arthritic body to come back after a million years or more. We make ourselves cheap in religion when we put too much value on this flesh. We become very cheap, small-minded.

Religion prepares people for life after ignorance

A great philosopher in Islam said to G_d, "Allah, my Lord, if You have nothing for me but what You have given me already I am already in heaven and I'm pleased." That is the kind of mind you have to come to and then you are freed from that small thing. No one can say it is not going to be for those people whose bodies have gone; that they are not going to have a second life. We can't say that. Don't ever say that, because you don't know that and Allah did not reveal religion to prepare people for life after the grave, that kind of grave. He revealed religion to prepare people for a life after ignorance, after blindness to what is truth and reality. He is a loving G_d and He accepts that. He says of that, "No one has seen or heard". But He did not say you won't have it, you won't get it. He gives us hope and faith and He gives us guidance for al-Akhirah, and faith and hope for that life when this is rotten and gone. He also gives us a bit of logic. He says He creates and repeats His creation and they say, "How is that?"

These are people who didn't believe there would be anything and that material death just finishes everything. So what does the revelation come to say to them? They say, "When we are dry bones, flesh all gone from the bones, how is there going to be a resurrection, a life after that?" Then Allah revealed to Muhammed (the prayers and the peace be on him) to say, "Not only when all your flesh is gone and you're only dry bones that He can put flesh on them, again, but He can even put the prints in your fingers, again". That is giving me the world of science. Long after Muhammed they established that my identity can be proven by my fingerprint. They are having a little trouble with it now but it is still working. They have not put it down. You do something wrong and have to be locked up and they are going to get that fingerprint. He (G_d) says He will bring back even your fingerprints. Isn't that something? We are given hope but Islam is not guidance for believing you're going to come back like that.

A new kingdom on this earth

G_d is going to bring truth and reality back, perfectly, better than it ever has been in the life of man and a ruling order will form in such light that will be just, very beautiful and productive, a new kingdom on this earth. It is coming. And it is going to be very beautiful and productive where you won't have to worry about harm coming to you from the government or from your neighbors; a world of righteousness, justice and beauty here on this earth. If we don't want to work for that then we're not true to the best spirit and urges in human life or in human nature. If we are true to that then we will live and do the best we can while we live and we will die with that hope; and children will come behind us, pick it up and keep it going until man has established it for everyone on this planet earth. Allah is with us to have it established.

1

Adam: The First Father

Addressing the angels and referring to the respect that should be given to Adam in the form that G_d made him the ruler, a responsible ruler, responsible to His Creator, Allah says supporting Adam, "When I give him from My Spirit make sajdah to him." When we orientate ourselves in our prayer facing the Ka'bah we are making sajda (prostration) to Adam. We are making sajda to the model that Allah wants for human excellence, or for human excellence on this planet earth; a model for all human life to emulate, to follow.

The first man created was our father, Adam, and what happened to him? First, let us go to the Bible. G_d caused him to go into a deep sleep. He was made but G_d caused him to go into a deep sleep. We think that just says we should picture a man alive walking about and then suddenly he falls down and goes to sleep. Actually, G_d caused him to go to sleep to his perception. G_d wanted him to go to sleep to his own perception.

When we close our eyes we dream. We can't command our thinking. We have also a dreamer in scripture who said he received a dream. It was no ordinary dream. This is me speaking in the language of the Bible, not my language. He received a dream that gave him guidance. He woke up from his dream and he realized that dream was a message from G_d and G_d wanted him to do something. So dreams come on different levels, not just the ordinary level of the common person going to sleep dreaming. It comes on a higher level than that, for guidance can come to you while you are asleep in your dream.

Adam fell into a deep sleep so he would not be in charge of his own mind, his own thinking. G_d made him dependent solely upon G_d. He didn't have power to think the way he wanted to think. His mind was out of his hands. G_d took his mind out of his control and G_d said, "It is not good that the man should be alone". So then He took from man a rib and from the rib of the man He made his mate, a woman.

Whatever the prophets have spiritually we all have

G_d made the community from a rib. I didn't say woman. I didn't say female. I said community. G_d made the community from a rib of man, because a rib is an arc or part of a circle. A curved line, if you keep extending it, what did Einstein say would happen? It comes right back to itself. If you keep extending it, it will complete the circle. So the curved line will eventually give you a full circle. And what is the full circle? The universe, everything. So it is just a hint or a sign of universality, universal knowledge, universal perception, where man makes connections by studying the whole system that G_d created; the whole system of matter. He makes connections and comes to a whole and he has a whole knowledge instead of part knowledge, or a piece of knowledge.

The Prophet (Muhammed) was lifted up from Masjid al-Haram where the Ka'bah is, into the heavens and he saw the prophets in graduations. On the first level was our father, Adam. Then on the second level he saw prophets John and Jesus. On the third level he saw the prophet, Yusuf, Joseph. And on the fourth level he saw the prophet, Idris. Some scholars say this is Ezekiel. On the fifth level he saw the prophet, Aaron, Haroon. On the 6th level he saw the prophet, Moses, the liberator; and on the seventh level he saw our second father, the prophet, Abraham, or Ibraheem. He greeted them each according to how we're supposed to greet them; as brothers, except the first one and the last one. But if I greet someone as brother that means they belong to the same flesh I belong to. It is saying, "Whatever he has in him as a mortal, I have". They are not different from each other as mortals. Whatever any of those prophets have in the seven ascensions, the seven levels of the ascent of man, spiritually, all of us have that in us.

Seven above you and seven within you

You have all of those prophets in yourself. They are in our own nature and capacity. What were they able to do? They were able to pick up things and receive revelation. That is saying we all have that ability; that even though G_d did not call us to use our ability for any particular purpose, inherently, we all have this. The Qur'an makes it very clear but most of us do not get it. It says there are seven tracts above you and a like number within yourselves. That is Qur'an. That is not me talking. I did not say a word. I only said what Allah revealed to Muhammed, the Prophet. There are seven above you and seven within yourself. So Allah did not reveal a religion that is foreign to our nature.

Allah revealed a religion that is our nature. Just like from a seed you get a plant, Allah can reach us through ourselves and other things that He created.

We all are connected no matter how many of us there are. We know that we have our mother and father in us and we know they have their parents in them and it goes back and back to the first one. So that is why the genealogy of Jesus Christ in the Bible is traced back to Adam and it says, "Who was created by G_d". So his genealogy, lifeline, goes all the way back to the first man. That is to say he is the type of the common life of people that G_d wants in all of us. That is what Jesus Christ is. In fact, all the prophets that we have are models of what Allah has put in every human being of our original nature and these types spread.

Scriptures say we should be looking at human types

We know we spread. All of us individually, bodily, physiologically, biologically, whatever you want to say, came from our parents. We know that. But when you read the sacred, Holy Scriptures, not just Qur'an, they say you should not be looking at physical bodies. You should be looking at human types. The types are not that many. If you would list all the different types, all the derivations, all the forms, or types derived from these native ones, the major types are not that many. And they boil them all down to three or four in religion. The minimum number is two, then three. First it is one, then, two, three, then four; and it goes up to about fourteen or fifteen. That is about it. Really, it stops at the number seven, like the seven heavens and after that it is like repeating one of those major types. So there are not that many types.

Religious science

When they say, "Seven", they put a lot of importance on the seventh son, saying, "Oh, he is the seventh son." There are not a lot of types. From those major types many other types come, innumerous types. You can't count them all. There are many types that come from the major types. When we think of the generation of Adam we should think of types and mainly the seven. The Prophet is the last to bring it all together in unity and make it have sense, clarity and have application in the real world. This is religious science.

We are told that Allah made from one soul its mate and from those two many others. So those are the two major types, two major patterns and from those two He made all the men and women. Those two in their origin were the same. But when they separated and were made to mate with each other, then, they had differences. One was like an anchor to hold life to the original pattern and nature. The other one was to go off from it to experience and develop his ownself, but also the world, to make an environment for his family. That is man.

Up straight in your soul and intellect

There is the word, "Qaamah". It means to stand up straight. The order to stand up straight is the word, "Qom." To please the meaning in that word if you slouch, it is not "qom". It is only when you are straight up. If someone is cripple where they can't stand up straight, nobody is going to bother them. It is understood that that is the best they can do. It is okay. There is no criticism at all. We're talking about language. We want to understand language. The language refers to, "up straight". But is it talking about "up straight" in your physical body? No, it's talking about up straight in your higher and more important life. That is the life of your soul and your intellect.

Standing up straight is a wonderful feat in itself, like the baby standing up for the first time. It gives you such a thrill to see the baby that was crawling standing. And the first time you see it standing it is such a thrill, not only for mothers but for fathers, too. It is a great thrill. The baby has been crawling and trying to pull up on something and then you see it standing. The expression on his face says he is balancing himself. He is afraid he is going to fall and he is looking at you as if to say, "Do you see me?" Maybe it can't talk but it is looking at you and saying, "You see me? I'm doing it?" It is a wonderful thing, standing up. And it is a spiritual balance, a spiritual feat for the baby just to stand up for the first time. It takes great spiritual tenacity. You have to hold it all together in a powerfully concentrated effort.

The religion of origin

Those philosophers and scholars who studied things that occur in the life of people to progress them for the good of mankind they read into all of these things and the Qur'an gives man his best language back. It gives man his best insights back. If man were able to find what G_d put in creation for him do you think G_d would ignore what man had found and give him something different or something more and not even mention what man has found, already? No, G_d gives man the best of what he finds.

"Deen al-fitral laahel latee fataran naasa 'alayha, the religion of origin upon which He fashioned mankind". All the societies of mankind, or the communities of mankind, that is what it means. Allah is telling us very clearly, "This is not a religion brought from outside of you. This is a religion that has been expressed from within you" and G_d is verifying and accepting the best that you have expressed of yourself.

Everything is real

There was no seventh heaven until Abraham got there. Does that make sense? When he got there then there was a seventh heaven, meaning that is the highest the human being can go in his spiritual ascent. So man had already gotten there. Then, G_d revealed the seven heavens to those who didn't know; for those who do not know and would not know if G_d had not inspired another man to see where Abraham went and how far he ascended; another man to understand these ascensions and describe them for us. This is nothing spooky. There is no superstition in al-Islam. It is all reality. Maybe we can't understand it all because our creation is limited. We are not G_d, so we can't understand it all, maybe. But there is nothing that is not real. Everything is real. G_d is real. The angels are real. Hell is real. This is al-Islam. I'm not talking from my head. I'm talking from what I've learned of al-Islam. Everything is real.

G_d has made nothing and nothing exists that is incompatible or foreign and can't be embraced by the five senses and human intelligence, even G_d. We can't see Him, directly, with our intelligence. But, we can see Him with our intelligence. He never said you couldn't see Him. He said, "You can't see Me, directly". You need references in creation to see Him. But you can see Him. Why would the scripture say, "Every eye shall see Him"? And why would man long in his soul and in his heart to see his Creator? Wouldn't his Creator be cruel to put that nature in his heart and in his mind and not answer what he wants? That would be a cruel G_d. G_d is a compassionate, merciful, loving G_d. I see Him better than I see you and I'm not exaggerating.

Moving to reach its divine purpose

Seratal mustaqeem is talking about our soul, its intelligence and the urge, the Will of G_d that is in it. Everything that G_d created His Will is in it. That is why it is given in this way. It says, "He has given something of His Spirit to everything." His Spirit means the direction for His Will. The flow, or direction of His Will, that is His Spirit. So if you're not in accord with His Will and you have used His creation in an improper way, what you used is going to be against you in the final Day of Judgement. Qur'an says your hand will speak out against you. The eye, every member of your body will speak against you saying, "He used me. She used me." Why? It is because the Will of G_d is in everything that He created. Everything from Him has His Will or something of His Spirit and His Will is a moving will. That is what spirit means. It is moving for its purpose, to reach its divine purpose.

The seratal mustaqeem is standing upright. Mustaqeem tells us of its path. Its path is not a path going horizontal like traffic does on the earth with streets and animals moving about. It is not going like that. It is going straight up. Its path goes straight up. To say, "Straight up", in Arabic, it is pronounced, "Astaqim". That is the language of the young fellows on the street saying, "Straight up, man!" But this very word, nothing added to it or taken away, was given to a man who came up to Muhammed, the Prophet. He said, "What can you tell me that no one else can tell me?" He (Muhammed) said, "Say, 'I have believed' and thereafter, istaqeem, be upright." But it is straight, be straight up.

Now he was telling that guy, "You are coming to me crooked and you haven't really accepted faith like you should, coming to me this way. Now you go back". As Christ, peace be on the Prophet, told Nicodemus, "You have to be born, again. You are not ready yet". Prophet Muhammed, in a way, was saying the same thing to him. "You have to be born, again. First, say, 'I have accepted faith' and thereafter be straight up".

Qur'an puts emphasis on thinking

So long before the world of philosophy and sciences that we know thinking men read into the ability to stand up straight, before the prophets. Before the prophets there were people called seers and at the same time they were called thinkers. That is why the Qur'an puts emphasis on thinking. It goes back to the earliest name or description of this activity in man that brings him to enlightenment. And the earliest are those who devoted themselves to thought, thinking on matters of importance in creation to understand, "How this is formed? How should I relate to it? What is my purpose in it?" These are the kinds of questions that the mind was asking. These men who asked such question (and some of them were women) they were blessed to come to see the light of G_d's Will in matter, in creation, in people and in everything.

This desire or this appetite in us is to become universal, to embrace everything, all sciences, all knowledge, etc. But how does it happen? It happens by observing the signs in creation. The bird flies high and can see a broader field or area on the ground like eagles and other birds that fly high. But the eagle is the one that is most known to fly high and have great, strong, powerful vision and can see little animals from that distance. If you were up there as high as the eagle you probably couldn't see a thing. But that eagle sees something running around down there and he will come swooping down like a dive bomber.

A life growing vertical

Men, thinkers, observing these things are the ones who gave this description to the higher life; that it is a life that goes vertical, straight up, to see better and to see more. The movement is towards the higher regions. By men going up on the mountain they found out that when you get up on the mountain the air is lighter, cleaner; and water that melts from ice on the mountain and comes down tastes better, cleaner and everything. So all these things that they experienced of the higher regions brought them to say man is aspiring to go in that direction, in the direction of purity, in the direction of broader vision. All of that became heaven. So they gave the name, "heaven", to all of that. Heaven simply means an elevation, a higher elevation.

In the study of man's soul and spiritual life the religious teachers and wise people are the ones who gave the meaning to the higher life as a life standing vertical, a life growing vertical (siratal mustaqeem). Now, it says the likeness of your creation is the creation of plants. This is G_d speaking in Qur'an. Most plants go straight up. A blade of grass goes straight up. That is to tell you that it is similar to your nature and the higher they go the more developed, the more complex, the more their life is fulfilled. If you catch them low down here they haven't realized their life, most of them. But as they get higher they realize their life, to produce flowers, to produce seeds, to produce fruits. Some trees they produce mostly wood, but they just get higher and higher until they reach their maturity.

Cain the industrialist

So this upward movement brought those who name things. Now this is not the bad Adam. This is the good one. The bad Adam is the one who was deceived to go astray from his natural orientation, or his firtra. The ones I'm talking about now they are not the bad ones. These are the good sons, children of Adam, who gave these names to things. Don't think that I'm saying that the Adam, who was deceived, gave names to everything. No, the Adam who was not deceived also give names to things. But the business world, the world of commerce, is the world of the Adam that went for the material things. If you want to look at the Bible I would say the world of commerce, or the children of Cain. And the world of faith is the children of the one called Abel, the community man.

Satan, he worked with Cain. He deceived Adam and worked with Cain; not the good Cain, the bad Cain. In fact, understand, too, these are types. So you can't say he's European. It so happened that the West excelled in modern history, but you can't make a race or anything out of these people. It is the human type and it's the production, the work. You can't identify it as any particular race because maybe it will be this race for this period in history and another race in another period in history. That would be the wrong way to identify them.

The path of purpose and ascension

In science they call it, "The ascent of man", not this religious man. You will get that in college if you haven't gotten it already in high school. You will get this language, "The ascent of man".

It is in dictionaries and encyclopedias. You can read about the ascent of man and they are talking about all people on this earth, not just one. This is a vertical path. The path of purity is the vertical path, the path of innocence, the path of purity, the path of purpose. Lastly, I said, purpose, because it is hidden in most of us. We don't know the purpose. We are wondering, "Why am I here? Why am I blessed to have all this?" You want to understand it. So purpose is usually the hidden thing that you come upon. But before you engage or focus on purpose you are already ascending because you have a natural desire just to be better. Your fitraa (original human design) is pushing you up straight.

Ascending results in more purity and leaves more indecency beneath you. Rise above indecency towards more justice, to be fair by yourself and fair by others. Just by being fairer in the way of your own life you are ascending. You ascend and ascend and you reach a height where you can no longer accept that you be that far away from the job that needs to be done on earth, i.e., people suffering needlessly, people being ignorant. So G_d doesn't have to send you back down. The same thing that sent you up is going to send you back down.

Everything that is ordered up there has peace. "Peace it is until the break of day or the rising of the dawn, the spread of the dawn" (Qur'an). So now you come back down. You're not in that peaceful region anymore. You're down here on earth where there is a lot of trouble and you have a purpose to fulfill. You have a job to do and the earth is not ready for it. So look at the danger that is involved. This is where religion starts. The religious mission, the progress of religion starts, now, where you are down here with your fellow man. Your ascending put you all the way up in the darkest regions of the universe and up there you saw the stars, the many lights. There is only one in the day. That is the sun. There is one major light and that is the sun. And the moon is seen sometimes in the day but its place is not there. You can hardly see it. It is a little dim light accompanying the sun in the day time. You go up there and see the many lights and the night is so beautiful.

So you have to march against that which G_d does not approve of. Man comes back down to do his job, to answer his purpose, his calling that is on earth, not up in the sky. But he had to go up there to prepare his soul and his spirit to deal with the matters down here.

Satan blinded by exaggerated perception of himself

Satan deceived our first father, Adam, the first, original type that gives birth to all other types. When he deceived him he told him in the Bible, "Don't be afraid to do this, You have misunderstood G_d. So take this that I'm offering you and you will become as G_d and the angels". This is the one who exaggerates his own creation. This is Satan, Shaitan. That exaggerated perception he has of his own creation is what blinds him to the light. Light not only helps you see. Light also blinds you if you get too much of it in your face, or eyes. That is a sign from the Creator, too.

You should not want the light for the light's sake. But want the light for how it can reveal what is in the dark. You are not supposed to go up to the sun to see it better. You are supposed to look at what the sun is shining on and see those things better. Satan, he wants to see the sun. He is more interested in seeing the sun because he wants to have the power of the sun. It is Satan who wants to see G_d. He does not want to see the light of G_d and what it shines on. No, he wants to see G_d, Himself, like the source of our day is the sun. Imagine, now, the sun as a meaning, or metaphor that is for G_d and he wants to now go and see the sun and analyze the sun. What is behind that kind of interest? It is a desire to be the sun, a desire to be G_d and that is what the scripture says of Satan, Shaitan. That is what the Bible says and if you understand it the Qur'an is verifying it; that he has in him that desire and he doesn't know it. He thinks he is a good servant of G_d. I've seen human beings like this on this earth in my lifetime.

He thinks he is a good servant of G_d. He is self deceived, self deluded. He thinks he is a good servant of G_d so he pursues this. He keeps going that way and what you think is G_d he doesn't even accept it. To him it is nonsense. It is not reality. This is Shaitan, Satan. So he doesn't respect our G_d. That is why they came out in the *Life Magazine* forty years or more ago and on the headlines of the magazine it said, "G_d Is Dead." There is no way a normal, natural human person could publish that in some paper, because the innocent are going to see that. The ignorant are going to see that and if it is on the headlines of the magazine he already can't understand religion that much anyway. So that is probably going to free him up to say, "I'm through with religion. Did you read the paper? It says, 'G_d is dead', man." I'm sure that was the reaction of a lot of youngsters and old people who had given up, anyway, on G_d and religion. The people who did that they are the Satan. They are the followers of the Satan, the Shaitan.

The biggest caption on the magazine I can see it right now, "G_d is dead!" Now if you mean something else you don't say it in bold letters like that on the paper. Say, "We're losing faith" and then in the article say, "G_d is dead in our life". It means in our mind G_d as a purpose and an interest is gone, dead. But, no, they knew what they were doing. They were preparing the human scene for their further exploits. They knew they were going to help many people say, "I don't need to be taking these matters seriously anymore". I do believe that article, that caption, made a lot of people give up on religion as a serious matter. They didn't stop there. They brought this little guy, who I liked, out in this movie. He was a good actor, George Burns. He was in a movie, *"Oh G_d"* and the second one was, *"Oh G_d! You Devil!"* Just that language says to the ignorant masses who are many in religion and out, "You don't have to take this religious stuff so seriously, man."

That is climaxing their work to discredit G_d and get you to relax and say, "I don't have to take this religious thing seriously. The expression, "G_d damn!" came from him, too. So it is a curse word. It was made a curse word. They knew it was going to be a curse word. They inspired it into the people and they knew it was going to be a curse word. It goes along with "m.f." and all those other words. Do you see the context they put G_d in? That is the Satan.

Connected with G_d in soul and spirit

These people have been around here longer than printed scripture. These devils have been on this earth planning to rule the human family for their own security and benefit. They were here long before any print or any ink was put on the paper to tell somebody what is revealed, or what is from G_d. This is no new thing. It is an old thing.

Just like G_d has created us to search for Him and His guidance and the way to know our purpose, those who follow the Satan they are searching, too. But they are searching with selfish interests like Satan and they are not connected, directly, with any ruler who is called Satan. However, they too, have the same powers that he has as intuitive powers. By intuition and powers of the intellect they connect with their ruler. They don't have to be connected with him, physically. We're not connected with G_d in that sense. We're connected with G_d in our soul and spirit. They connect with the Satan's cause. We connect with G_d's cause because that is what we want in our nature. They connect with Satan's cause because that is what they want in their nature.

So they become a powerful force of the devil, Satan and all his little followers who have connected into his energy. They have connected into his energy like we connect into the energy of G_d, His will, His Spirit, etc. So you see this thing is big. It is real. It is more real than what we see that's not real.

Ascending for spiritual excellence

The path is vertical, man's ascending upward. That means it is the path of his excellence in his spiritual soul and spiritual body. The path of virtues and principles, righteousness and purity, innocence and justice, that is the vertical path. We can only ascend along the path of our progress for our soul and intellect. We can only ascend so high and the burden is going to get so heavy on us from down here. The misery down below is going to bother you so much you're going to have to come down from heaven or down from the mountain and do your job; and it is not going to be easy. "Peace it is until the rise of the dawn, or the spread of the dawn."

Addressing the angels and referring to the respect that should be given to Adam in the form that G_d made him the ruler, a responsible ruler, responsible to His Creator, Allah says supporting Adam, "When I give him from My Spirit make sajdah to him." When we orientate ourselves in our prayer facing the Ka'bah we are making sajda (prostration) to Adam. We are making sajda to the model that Allah wants for human excellence, or for human excellence on this planet earth; a model for all human life to emulate, to follow.

It is recorded also and we know these familiar words, "Adam was created on the pattern of 60 arm spans". Further, the Prophet said, "No one dies or is resurrected except on that pattern." For those of you most of whom came from church leadership in your life, we know that Christ Jesus is given as a sign of the resurrection and the resurrection, itself. He is a personification, a picture of the resurrection, itself. And we know that it is said in the Bible of Jesus Christ that he is the son of Adam. We know he is the son of the word. He is the son of the spirit. He is created, that is, the spirit and the word of G_d. In our religion we don't say, "Son", because it is an offence in our language. It is a serious offence to say that he is the son of G_d. We understand that language to mean that G_d created him as He created Adam and he had no existence before G_d created him. Therefore, Jesus had no existence before G_d created him and He created him as He created Adam.

Adam not the son of a man but the creation of G_d

The Bible supports this position that is taken in al-Islam. If you read in the Bible, the genealogy of Christ Jesus saying where his life came from it goes back to Adam and the Bible says, he (Adam) was created by G_d. So it goes back to the first father and it is said of the first father he was created by G_d. So that establishes a line of reasoning that says in the Bible that Jesus is the son of Adam. By reasoning that identifies him as the extension of the first Adam, the first father and that father was not the son of man. That father was the creation of G_d.

Adam has not passed away. He is in all of us. So if Adam has a possibility to become Christ then that possibility also is in all of us. So let us not continue to be burdened by mysteries. This is the time of transparency for religious people. We should not be burdened by mysteries. It is time for all to come where Prophet Muhammed and before him, Prophet Jesus, were established to take us. It is time to be there, now. All the prophecies point to this time. This is the fulfillment of all the great issues in scripture. When will the time come if not now? Never! This is the time and all the signs point to this being the time. All the signs in scripture point to the great workings that we see in the world to bring man home to the destiny for his human excellence.

Religion comes to liberate civilization

So I return now to the language in the hadith, or the sayings of our Prophet, that Adam was created on a pattern of sixty arm spans. Why arms? It is because we work with arms and the arm supports our hand that does the delicate and skilled work as well as the manual labor. The hand writes, records and saves the precious information in history to pass it on to the coming generations. But the hand also does skilled labor, runs very complicated machines and does very complicated things in industry. The hand is skilled and it is supported by the arm. The same arm will use what the hand has done and can use it as a force to advance society, to advance civilization, defend society, or to defend civilization. We say, Armed Forces, military.

"On a pattern of sixty arm spans", that is far reaching that saying of the Prophet that no one is resurrected except on that pattern. So what is that plainly telling us and the son of Elijah Mohammed can give it to you? It is plainly telling us that religion comes to better civilization and to liberate even civilization when it becomes stagnant. When it stops and can't see any way to continue in the road of progress for human society, then religion comes to give it life again and to put the world back on the road to civilization. What did a wise reformer say who came to the black bottoms of Detroit among the poorest of the black people? He said, "The duty of a civilized person is to teach the uncivilized." No doubt then that sixty arm spans refers to the community's social life and social consciousness.

2

Abraham: The Imam for All Nations

So let us try to see our religion not only with our heart and with our sensitivities but let us see our religion with our rational mind. Abraham, our second father, he is a sign of the excellence of the human brain and intellect. The Promised Land that is associated with this father of ours, it is education supported by natural creation, the sciences and all of the other beautiful things that come out of the search for better life through the nature of the material world, or the order of the material world. Scientists are born when they give themselves to this focus.

From the heavens comes perception. How are we to pinpoint this so we know, in fact, what this is all about? The Prophet, Abraham, is our second father. He is called the second father because he earned it from G_d. G_d saw him in his constitution, in his mental makeup, in his mind, his thoughts, his interest, and what his heart was interested in. G_d loved him in that form and even called him a friend, "Khalilulaah". And G_d gave him the title, "Imam for all nations, for all people". According to Prophet Muhammed, G_d also established him as our second father when he reported it to his following and to the world what he experienced on his ascent from the Ka'bah up into the heavens and his night travel from the vicinity of Mecca, the Ka'bah, to the distant mosque, Al Aqsa. He reported what he saw.

When he (Prophet Muhammed) was taken up he saw Adam, our first father, on the first level. In his ascending up into the heavens he greets him to let us know how we are to recognize Adam. He said, "Peace be on you, my father, Adam". On every other level he ascended to he met the prophets and he would greet them the same way. But he would not say, father. He said, "My brother, this is my brother", that until he reached the 7th Heaven and he met Abraham there. He greeted him also, as father. He said, "Peace be on you, my father, Abraham". You will not find this in the Qur'an. This is given so that we will know that we are, as followers of Prophet Muhammed, to recognize Jesus Christ, Adam and all the others, and the last in the seventh, highest heaven, Abraham. We are to recognize and know that two of those are the fathers of mankind; the first one, the mortal, Adam and the last one, the intellect, Ibraheem (Abraham).

How did the sky serve Abraham? Abraham was trying to find truth to free his heart and his soul and put his mind in a situation to grow so it would please him. The thinkers, we call them free thinkers in the history of the development of the world. The free thinker is pondering or thinking on what he is observing in the real world, everything in his environment including himself. He is thinking, "How did this come about and what is the purpose of this?" He wants understanding for his mind and his soul. Abraham left his own father because he was worshiping things that the young Abraham couldn't accept. Abraham followed common sense. It told him that those things that his people made should not be authorities in his life and he shouldn't trust those things that his people made with their hands and called gods. He shouldn't trust them with his hopes, his wishes and his life. Actually, he destroyed the idols, broke them up, and his father heard that his son did that. So he went to his son and he said, "Did you do this, Abraham?" Abraham said, "Ask the biggest one who did it". So his father was very much insulted. His patience quickly ran its course and he told his son, "Get out! You are banished from this kingdom. You cannot stay in this kingdom."

G_d was freeing Abraham

So he drove him out of the kingdom that he was in. He had to go to other countries and really I think that was the way G_d freed him. That was His first step for freeing him. G_d wanted to put him out of his own land and make him go where strangers lived. So he went into strange lands and everywhere he went he was truthful, honorable and upright. This is the Bible.

One day, according to the Qur'an, he was searching the outer boundaries of the universe, of the creation, to see if he could find, "What should I recognize as G_d?" You know how the story goes, some of you. When night fell he saw the stars and they were all beautiful and appealing to him. But once he saw a star fall, he said, "No, stars cannot be my G_d because G_d does not fall." Now he hadn't actually met with G_d, yet, but the human being is given common sense and it told him, "I shouldn't worship something that's dying, falling out of the sky, light going out". He wanted something that would stay lit, eternally, that would serve him, eternally, because he was not just looking for something for his own life. He was looking for something that would serve mankind, forever, on this planet earth. So he rejected the stars as being G_d.

He stayed until the night passed and the sun started to rise. Its light, from our situation as human beings, seems so much nearer. It seems so much bigger and the sun seems so much bigger than the objects out there afar. Because they are so far away, they appear to be smaller than our sun. Science has revealed to us and we know there are objects out there much bigger than our sun. But we can't know that with the ordinary vision or the human eye. We have to have telescopes and scientific thinking to discover that. The sun came up big and he said, "Look how splendid this one is rising in its glory; how bright and beautiful." He continued to watch it. It rose up until noon day and started to decline. It declined and it went out. Then he said, "I witness that the One behind all of this is G_d. None of this world is G_d but there is Something behind it. Something started all of this and that is G_d". Jews and others, especially Jews and Muslims, we recognize that Abraham is the one who came to the conclusion that the Creator or the Cause behind creation, the Maker of all this, is the only G_d; one G_d alone.

Shirk oppresses the intelligence

So he (Abraham) gave us the monotheistic idea in religion. When he gave us that he gave us much more than that. He gave the world much more than just the belief that there is one G_d. Allah says surely worshiping more than one with G_d, confusing the idea of G_d, putting something with G_d, making Jesus Christ, the Prophet, or Messenger, a god, surely this is the worst form of oppression. What is it oppressing? Number one, it oppresses your intelligence and your good senses. It's going in conflict with the common good sense that G_d gave you. It's in conflict with the intelligence G_d gave you. G_d created my common sense to know that this is hot. This is cold. This is dangerous. This is ugly. This is beautiful. This is hard. This is soft. This is intelligent. This is not G_d. He gave every human being this sense. Now when something goes against that sense you shouldn't accept it. I don't care what it is. If it is Imam W. Deen Mohammed and he goes against your good common sense, you shouldn't accept what he says that goes against your good common sense. But don't reject it just instantly thinking, "That's wrong". No, because you could be wrong. But after you discuss it with others who have good common sense and others you respect as intelligent and you come up with a decision that this is against good common sense, you should reject it. I don't care where it comes from.

Again, when G_d says, "Surely associating or confusing the idea of G_d is the worse form of oppression", what is being oppressed? Your intelligence, your brain, your good senses are being oppressed. If I can enslave your brain I can enslave everything else you have. So the way to free a person is through the brain and the way to enslave a person is through the brain. You can't enslave me until you have my brain. You might lock me up and put shackles on me, but I'm not a slave.

Hemlock or blood lock

The best part of me escapes shackles. It reaches out beyond prison walls and many men have been put in prison and have come up with their best production while they were locked up. They wrote their best works and left humanity that which will advance humanity though they died in prison. Socrates was one of them. They arrested him and eventually killed him by poisoning him. They gave him hemlock. What is hemlock? It is blood lock. What is blood lock? Blood lock is mind lock. So what was the real death of Socrates? They prevented him from using his intelligence and passing his intelligence on to others. They locked it up so it could not get out to others. That was his real death. That was the worst thing they did to Socrates and that is how you should understand the crucifixion of Jesus Christ. They gave him aceta (vinegar). This is the New Testament and it says as soon as he drank the aceta, right away he gave up the spirit, the ghost, and he was dead.

Aceta is a play on asceticism. This is the way you have to understand these things and if you understand them this way you will be free indeed. You will then be in good position to have a good and pleasant life. Your life will be relieved of a lot of unnecessary burden, like that which weighs down the back, a load the animals carry. But the animal never sees the load. He just feels it on his back. Some of the drug addicts say, "I'm carrying a monkey on my back."

Abraham is correct thinking for the free thinker

It was Abraham who really liberated mankind and here he is not a human person. Abraham is a correct thinking for the free thinker personified in Abraham. He is a personification of the activities in the mind of the free thinker who will take the world where it has to go, rationally, intellectually and spiritually speaking. When you see the whole universe then you say, "This earth is small. This is just a small thing in this big creation, or this big reality." Then you become less home oriented. You become less oriented as a member of a nation. Your nationality becomes less important to you now than your new perception of truth and reality. Not only your nationality but your tribe, your race, all become less important to you, now, than your new perception. If all of us can see what liberates all human minds and hearts, we can agree in that one thing and it is bigger than all of our small things, because this is the universe, not America, not the United States. This is not London. This is the universe we are talking about. It is much bigger than all of us. So if we can agree in what this bigger reality is saying in its speech to our intelligence and we can all come together, this brings us to the next connection that all agree in one pattern, or one system, all of these worlds. The earth by itself is so small, like a speck that you can't find with your naked eye. In the system of matter, or the worlds, you can't find the earth unless you have a telescope. But if you're far enough away, you can't find the earth with the most powerful telescope that is in existence. This is the reality.

One life in common

This little small world that we live on, this small space that we occupy here that we call earth, it has its systems, not one system. It has a system of material things, also, systems of energy. There are two main realities, material and then energy. It has another reality designed because this matter has design. The design of one metal will be different from the design of another. But the design of matter is one. They have one common design like we have one common human life. When you get hurt and you need blood the doctor is not going to ask, "What is your race? I've got some Chinese blood here what is your race?" You don't need Chinese blood. You need human blood. You don't need African blood. You need human blood. The doctor is not going to ask you, "What is your race?" He is going to give you some blood and you're going to be all right.

We have one life in common, don't we? G_d has made us one life in common, so we have one pattern in common, one design in common. When you go with a broken bone to the doctor, he is not going to ask you, "What did you say you broke?" and you say, "I broke my left arm". That is enough. The doctor is going to that left arm. He's not going to treat you like you're an octopus. He knows you're not an octopus. You are a human being and he knows all human have the same left arm. So he will go to the chart and won't say, "Give me an Egyptian chart of the human anatomy". They are all the same for one man as it is the same for another no matter what part of the world he lives in. This is universal, like this is one single life. What I'm getting at is this. Just as we can find the true identity in one single pattern of life that makes us all the same species or the same human, flesh creation, we can find also the unity of matter that is true for all matter no matter where it comes from; out of the skies, down here, or anywhere. It is the same. What is that? The molecular construction, structure of matter is the same for all matter. All matter is composed or consists of molecules, electrons, protons, neutrons, etc. So we could come up with the anatomy of matter couldn't we? We can get beneath the covering of colors and racial differences. We can get beneath all that, beneath the outer flesh and come to the logic of how it is structured and the structure is the same for all. The same is true for the earth. If you can find the scientific key for unlocking matter you'll find what is true for matter everywhere.

The mind pictured as Abraham

The earth has all these various systems, system of rivers, of oceans, system of air. All of these are systems and then within these systems we find smaller systems. So there are a lot of systems. Then we study it as students of the mind and the world and we find that there is a science of skin, science of blood, science of everything in the human composition. We study the outer world and there is the science of geography, the science of geology, of astronomy, all these different sciences; and the one who started this process was Abraham. Go back to the meaning I gave you of Abraham as not a person. Don't look for a Jew and don't look for an Arab. Look for the description I gave you of Abraham. The human mind, pictured as Abraham, searched the existing world of reality to make sense of it and came to the conclusion that this is one system of logic. It is not in conflict with itself and that tells me that it could not have happened without a purpose and without it being designed that way, because I am a mind. I am human and this world feeds my mind and has fed my mind and shown me its unity. So my conclusion is there must be a living Reality behind it that is of a different nature and superior to it that caused it to exist; and He did it all for the human being, for His creation, so it would advance and have comforts unimaginable.

So the expression is, "He created man expressly for His mercy". I had this idea even when I was a young minister. Long before I came to this development I'm in now I had this mind. I started thinking on the so-called primitive people and how the Indians and some other primitive people have tried to show the evolution of man and put creatures on a totem pole showing a progression for life; that all these lives are in one stream or in one progression. This is a picture or diagram of something showing man's existence with all these other creatures and man ascends highest on the pole.

Philosophical thinking unfolds into exact sciences

Philosophical thinking is a forward step or progression that eventually unfolds into exact sciences. So I'm a man and I think and I have more freedom to think and there are more possibilities for me as a freethinker than it is for any other life that exists. I am made of the world. My living body is made of the world. It came from the world that G_d created. Then my mind is influenced by the world G_d created and it comes to life and starts to form and grow because of its feeding on the life that G_d created. I eat chicken and when I eat it, it has a chance to rise high, to the highest possibility for flesh or matter when it enters my matter. When the chicken becomes a part of my matter, now, he is in a situation that lifts him up to the highest possibility for living things. Can't you see how it is justified that G_d give us these things and that He says He created man for the world and the world for man? The world has no real purpose without man and man has no real purpose without the world. So if we look to make sense of things we can do it much better than anybody that is trying to do it without the guidance of G_d. In fact, we are the only ones that can do it. Now, I eat and what I eat makes, replenishes, the cells in my body. So you tell me this (my body) is not chicken? This is chicken, fish, lamb, vegetables, oxygen, hydrogen, etc. This is everything that comes into my body. So if G_d crowns the creation with me everything has been crowned or lifted into the seat, the throne, because of my existence.

If you can't follow that line of reasoning, then look at it this way. They can't appreciate each other and they can't appreciate their own existence. But G_d has created me to appreciate myself and all of them in a framework. That is wonderful and beautiful. So actually their reality remains low until man engages them in his thinking. So even if we can't see the material proof that these things have not been put down, they have been put on earth to be lifted up once they enter man; if you can't see that then see, at least, that by themselves they have no real exciting existence or glory. But when they come into the life of man and become a part of his world they are raised up in importance and value. Their meaning becomes so much greater. So everything is fed into the higher and that is intelligent man.

The house a metaphor of word of G_d

The expression, "Qawaa'id bait", gives us knowledge, not just imagination. When Abraham was building the house (Ka'bah) the term for how he was constructing it is, "Qawaa'id." The word that is used is the word for grammatical construction. The house is a physical picture, but the real meaning is not physical. The house represents language that Allah communicated to Abraham. So the house is a metaphor of the word of G_d. "In the beginning there was the word". Again, the house is a metaphor, a physical picture that you should not take as a physical house. But you should think on it. You should meditate on it. You should reflect on it. You should think deep into it. Now what does it look like? It looks like a little small cubicle and if it is the first house why is it so small? It is because it is the first house. It is saying, "This is your beginning. You have a big house now. You have mansions but your beginning was from a little, small, simple house, a small simple structure; no furniture in it". How do I know? The rulers of Saudi Arabia took me and a few who were with me inside the Ka'bah and asked us if we wanted to pray in there. Do you know what I told them? I said, "I don't feel right praying inside the Ka'bah. Prayers are to be done outside".

Ka'bah not real house

It is not a real house. It is a sign that is imparting messages to the real thinker who G_d has blessed to be a thinker. So it is speaking of our beginning as a social body. Allah made people to be a social order. "How can you prove that?" He says we all came from one father and a mother. That is enough. That says it, that the origin, the beginning of human beings on this earth is a social order, socially related to one another; and you interact with each other upon respect for the relationship that you have with each other. Father and mother, parents and children, brothers and sisters, those are relationships and what Allah calls, the family ties. And He says reverence, have taqwa for G_d, but also have taqwa for the family ties. So what does it mean? If G_d says, "Have taqwa for G_d, for Me", and then He says, "Wal arham," meaning also the close ties of family; if He says that the word literally goes back to the womb of the female. It means the fruits of her womb and the fruits of her womb are the children that are produced by the father. So the common sense conclusion is that Allah is talking about family. But the way He communicates is most powerful and rich in broadcasting meanings, light and understanding.

Abraham had a partner in building house

Getting back to Abraham and building the house, let us now go from the building of the house to Abraham's son who helped him build the house. Abraham had a partner building the house and his partner was his son. Isn't that a beautiful picture? Such a great thing he was doing building a house that would be a sign communicating wisdom, faith and blessing to all mankind, built for all people and his son was working with him. Let us see how this son earned the right to help our father build such a marvelous and wonderful sign.

So we go to his son now and we want to review his son coming up from birth. The first thing we have to see to understand this son, Isma'il (Ishmael), is that his mother was a woman who had been put out, an outcast. High society rejected her and the high society that rejected her was the society of the accepted religious order in its highest recognition, or in the highest view we have of that community. The most respected of them rejected her and that is given in the name, Sarah, for Sarah was the wife of Abraham and he was the father of the order. Sarah asked him to, "Take my maid servant. I am too old to bear a child." He did it as his wife Sarah asked of him. He took Hagar for his wife, Hagar (Hajar in Arabic). As she began to show signs of pregnancy, Sarah began to get jealous. Abraham, naturally, his heart is the most excellent of human hearts, "Qalben salim." It means beautiful, safe from harming anybody; a beautiful heart of peace that has no ill will in it, or interest in it to harm anybody. So he is going to show kindness to Hagar and he is going to show more kindness and care as she becomes more burdened with child. But this made Sarah jealous. You ask, "How can this man talk like this as if he was there when it happened." G_d was there and He is always there at all times and all places. So whatever G_d wants His servant to know He just says, "Be and it is, Kun fa yakun." Actually, for me, I know I don't get any credit. My disposition is, "I know nothing. I have access to nothing. This is not my credit. This is Your credit, Allah", subhana wata alaa, highly glorified and praised is He.

Hagar denied a place like Mary and Jesus were denied

Sarah said, "Take this woman out of here. She cannot stay here!" So Abraham, with a heavy heart because he loved his wife, Sarah, with perfect love, took Hagar out into a desert place. What does that tell us? Much, but, I'm talking on the level that practically any common sense person can understand. That is where I am talking now. What does that tell us? When Mary, the mother of Jesus Christ, was carrying him, peace be on the two of them, there was no place for her to deliver her baby. Every place rejected her. They wouldn't accept her, so she ended up having to bear her child in a manger, a place where they kept animals, like a barn. The picture is a picture of a barn where the animals were kept. That is where she had to go and have her delivery. Now don't think there is no relationship or no connection that is very, very important for Mary's dilemma and desperate situation and that of Hagar and her baby. There is a direct and strong connection and actually the issue is repeated in the New Testament. The same issue that is in the Old Testament is repeated in the New Testament; the issue of discrimination and judging people by their physical or material status and by their situation under overpowering forces that deny them free expression, free exercise of their native talents that G_d created them with. The same issue comes up in the New Testament and it is given in the concept, or in the picture of Mary and her child that she was carrying. So that barren place, that desert, showed no cultural development, dead land. That barren place, arid land, dry land that is not producing anything, that land is where Abraham saw the marking, the Black Stone and the place for building the house for all people, for all mankind.

Running between two hills

Now his son, he is in that barren place and this is before the house was built. He is in his mother and she delivers him in that barren place, that nonproductive place, a garden with no fruits. She delivers him but she can't find water for her baby and he is thirsting for water. So she panicked, became very desperate. Panic means you lose you rational control and your mental control. Thoughts are not helping you. You just panic and you just go upon spirit or upon the force of spirit in you. And she went upon that, panicking as she ran between the two hills. She would run up one hill, Safa, and then she would run to the other hill, Marwa. Hills raise you up from lower levels and isn't that our natural spirit to go up to G_d? When you really desperately need G_d you raise your hands and you lift your head up saying, "Oh G_d! Oh G_d!" If there is a raised plain you want to get up higher. So she saw these two hills. She ran up to one screaming and pleading for help and she ran to the other. As soon as she got there she ran back, going backwards and forward. Isn't that the way the mind operates when you are trying to find a solution? It goes from one extreme to another. It goes to one extreme and it doesn't find an answer. Then it leaves that and goes to the opposite extreme. That is what we should understand, that this picture of what was happening to her is what happens in our mind when we are desperate to find an answer or solution because we need it, immediately. We need to find it in our mind, immediately. The situation is grave, so we start searching and we run in one direction in our mind and we don't find the help. Then we go in the opposite direction and can't find the help. So you keep running back and forth, back and forth. While she was doing that the Merciful G_d was working, too and He caused a well to spring up in dry land, in the desert. Isn't this beautiful? Yes, but look where it sprang up.

Water sprang up at his heels

This is how the story, the tradition, is given. It says a little bird came and pecked in a spot. As it pecked in that spot water began to ooze up to the surface. The water sprang forth and she was able to get water for her child. Where did the water appear? It appeared at the heels of Isma'il, at the baby's heels. She had put the baby down on the desert and she had run desperately trying to find help, trying to find, "Where is there water for my thirsting child?" So, she happened to look at the place where she left him while she was panicking and she saw water coming up at his heels from the ground. So she went there and she was able to get water. Now, that's the beginning of what? That's the beginning of the development of that barren area. The Arabs see that as the beginning of their life as a people. They became the people of the desert, the children of Isma'il, called Ishmael in the Bible. So they are the children of Ishmael. They are the children of Abraham, the father of Ishmael. They are the children of Hagar (Hajar), the wife of Abraham who gave birth to Ishmael. So they are the children of Hagar, also, and they called us (African Americans) Hagar's children.

Let me continue with the son of Abraham, peace be on them, the prophet and his son. Water sprang up at his heels. What does the heel mean? What do you rest on when you stand up? Your heels, don't you? You rest on your heels. So, the water springing up at his heels meant spiritual balance. Here is a son that G_d is giving Abraham who is going to be spiritually balanced. Abraham needed help from somebody like that. Why? It was because he was motivated by reason more than by soul or spirituality. That is why he asked certain questions of G_d like, "G_d, tell me how the dead are going to be raised."   When Isma'il grew up nobody had to explain to Isma'il how the dead would be raised, because he had already been dead and G_d raised him up from the dead, spiritually and gave him spiritual balance.

We died as mortals and then as thinkers

Isn't that what Allah says, that from the dead He brings forth the living? He brings the living out of the dead and that is what He has done for us. He brought the living out of the dead and now He's bringing the dead out of the living. We died twice, didn't we? We died as mortals and then we died as thinkers and we had to reject the dead matter that was in our thinking before. That is taking the dead out of the living. So Isma'il is a great sign, especially water coming up in a dead desert place at his heels. Now you know most of the leaders or thinkers in the religion, traditionally, they see that occurrence as the beginning of people's awareness and travel to that spot for water, but not for just ordinary water; for water seen as part of the ritual, or part of the rites of Hajj, the Zam Zam well.

Isma'il is spiritual balance

Again, we are called the children of Hagar and Abraham's son, Isma'il, is a picture of spiritual balance. I was saying that Abraham needed his son to help him structure the house, because Abraham tended to be inclined toward the rational more than the spiritual. He was so much inclined towards the rational because he saw the great future production for people who devote themselves to reason and to the rational for the material construction of the world. He knew how important that was. So it really bothered him that, "Now, I have a son and this son is devoted to the spiritual nature and I know G_d wants me to do what I'm doing. G_d wants me to build a society under Him, a world under Him and I am rational. We have to deal with the rational and material reality. This son of mine he may cause a problem. If he gets too many people into his spiritual mode we will have difficulty building a material society, an industrial world. G_d, this is my son and my thinking is telling me You want me to sacrifice him. I love him. This is my child. Lord, this is my child. Please, what am I going to do?" Allah would not speak to him.

So he went and got the knife. I believe it was a shining sword, illuminated sword. He got this illuminated sword and he was getting ready to kill his child and G_d said, "Do it not. You have already completed your commitment to Me. Your willingness to sacrifice him for My pleasure is enough. Instead of sacrificing him get that little innocent lamb, that sheep, and slaughter him with that knife you have. And when you kill it take all the stinky stuff out of him. Wash it up real good and then put it on the fire and cook it and let a sweet savor as steam and smoke go up to the heavens. Then serve it to the poor and you to eat from it, Abraham."

We have that ritual every 10th day of the Hajj (Pilgrimage), where we make our slaughter of a sacrificial animal. The best animal to have for the occasion is a lamb. You can have a cow or camel. They eat a lot of different kind of meats and they sacrifice them, too. But the best is the lamb because it is the most peaceful of all of them. What a beautiful story, I'm telling you, the scene where he is tormented in anguish, in agony and G_d relieves him by showing him what to do. Do you know the sheep and goat, too, these are the most sure footed of all animals. They can go up on ridges and stand on a little small stone and hold themselves right there; climb up on mountains and stand on real small ridges. So G_d removes from Abraham's vision his son and by some kind of activity in his mind there is an illusion and the son is replaced by the sight of a lamb. And by him seeing that in a day vision, he reasoned that G_d was saying, "No, don't kill your son, kill a lamb. Your son is innocent; innocent as a lamb".

Kill the tendency to tolerate abuses

"So don't kill him. Kill a lamb. Kill this tendency in your house, or in your following, to tolerate abuses and be eaten by other animals, hunted by other animals, and slaughtered by other animals. Get that out of your people, It's innocence this passive way of theirs. It is innocence but, Abraham, you are right. It is a problem for the work of establishing the new world under G_d. So tell them that this nature in them is to be digested by their minds and protected by their intelligence and their faith. Don't let your life become the life of sheep. But benefit from the life of the sheep by digesting the knowledge and wisdom. The sheep is peaceful and you are to be peaceful in accord with your best nature, your Muslim nature. The sheep likes to be with each other and you should be close to each other, like the sheep. And sheep do not like to engage in arguments and fighting. I want you to be like that, too. But if I command you to kill, I want you to stop being a sheep and be a man on the battlefront. So Abraham, teach them My signs that I put in the sheep. From the sheep you get wool and you can take the wool and protect yourself from the cold of night or winter. So you be like that. You produce that which will help the people, keep them warm on cold nights, or in the winter. You see all the beautiful signs? And the sheep is well balanced, like Isma'il. So tell them, not only your son, that they should all be well balanced, spiritually. Don't be too heavy on the left. Don't be too heavy on the right. Don't be too heavy forward. Don't be too heavy backward. But find the just mean for balance. Be hanifa, upright, erect, not inclined to go off from the balance, spiritually balanced."

A person who is spiritually balanced will stay rational. It is only the person who goes to spiritual extremes in one direction but is not circumspect, not respecting the whole situation all around that is a problem. So they are going off on a tangent from the mean, from the balance, or from the plummet line. You preachers out there, you're leaving the plummet line and going to extremes. But wasn't it G_d, according to the Bible, Who ordered the plummet and the plummet line?

Continuous stream of purity

Somebody may say, "When he starts saying that the Bible has a continuous stream of purity in it from Genesis to Revelation, he loses me. That is the poison book." With all this that G_d has shown me in the Bible I cannot disrespect that book. I would be a sinner to disrespect it and an ignorant person to disrespect it. If there comes a storm and the storm blows trash and dirt and the water rises so high that dirty, muddy water comes into the masjid under the masjid door are you going to throw the masjid away? You should clean the masjid up and make your salat (prayer). That is what Muhammed was guided to do by G_d; not to go and destroy churches and condemn the Christian people and prevent them from practicing their religion under his order or in the land of the Muslims. He did not prevent them. He saw the corruption. He saw the filth and there is filth in the Bible that is very embarrassing. But that was produced for the pagans who were a people who were vulgar; educated, but at the same time their fun was vulgarity, sexual indecency and vulgar display of their sexual interest. They were a people who prided themselves in being powerful as an army. So that instinct and that spirit in them to fight and kill was so strong and they took such pride in it that their sport was to put fighters against each other and actually fight to the death. There is much I have to say on that but we do not want to waste time.

Ka'bah sign of how to structure and serve society

The story and picture of Abraham and his son constructing the house should also be seen by us as what we need in us in order to be successful in structuring society and serving human society in the best way. We need people who are spiritually pure, spiritually balanced, to work with us who are doing the rational or material work. We need their input and their authority as well as that of the people who are more inclined or more orientated as industrialists or builders. The building has to include them both, because every people have their own qiblah. That is in the Qur'an.

Human form most excellent of forms in creation

It is said that one of the great khalifahs kissed the Black Stone. This is after the passing of the Prophet. He said, "If I hadn't seen the Messenger of G_d doing this I would not do this." Understand that the persons in the immediate association of Muhammed, the Prophet, were men who were called the hunafaa. They did not believe in superstitions. They only believed in what they could understand with their normal, rational minds. But they also believed that the human being's creation, the human form, among living things was the most excellent of forms. Any thinking person can come to that conclusion. You know we can do more with our minds than any other living thing. So we are the best and the highest of all living things on the earth. So that was their belief and the logic for their discipline is just that. Since I am the best then I should respect my form over all other living forms. I shouldn't behave like a dog. I am a higher creation than a dog or a higher form than a dog. So these were the hunafaa.

They were very intelligent people. So the companion of the Prophet saw himself above kissing the stone and he said, "I wouldn't do it if the Prophet himself had not done it". But now, if he was not from the Arab people and he had been from a

Christian land, or another part of the world where Christians had been established, he would not have had any trouble kissing the Black Stone if he accepted the Prophet, the Qur'an, and his leadership. These were Arabs who had not been Christians. The Christians were converted, too. They were there, too, making Pilgrimage. No Christians were having a problem like that because the Bible says, "And the rejected stone became the corner in the house".

Now if you understand building construction, masonry, which means building, what we call now the developer, the one who puts the house up; if you understand what the corner is, especially for back then, you form a right angle. That is the key. You form one right angle on the ground or dig a trench right angle. Once you do that you make a straight line from one side of that right angle to where you want it to go, or as far as you want it to go. You make it as long or as big as you want it and you stop. You take the other side of the angle and you stop. Now you have half of the square. So once you get the corner you can get the whole square building and the Ka'bah is square. Once you get one corner right all you have to do is line the other ones up with it. The other three sides are lined up with it and you have a perfect square for building the house.

The heart made a mistake

So the one corner is very important. The corner that you start with is very important. And the stone that fell represents the original nature of mankind that fell from heaven, not physically speaking, but ideally speaking. It is an idea that you are developing, not a physical structure. Once you get the corner lined up you've got it. The stone is black but it was not always black. It was shining white in the sky. It burned out and when it cooled it was black. What is this blackness? This blackness must be understood when we study the human heart. If you kill a person and take the heart out and let it cool off in time it will turn black. The blood turns black.

Really, for the Ka'bah that corner represents the human heart and it is good. The heart made a mistake, thinking it can go up above mortal life or flesh, carnal nature; go above it and become saintly, angelic, or divine. It made a mistake. So that passion for divinity has to burn out and that mind that thinks you are something special, not human like other humans, has to die. All of those messages are in a star, a lit body falling down here from the sky and cooling off.

When we look at it now it represents the heart and it did not have a silver ring around it. But the custodians of the Ka'bah put a silver ring around it. You who made the Hajj and kissed the Black Stone, or just passed by, maybe you didn't have a chance to kiss it, because sometimes they rush you and you can't get to it. If you saw it, you saw a corner with a stone in there with a silver ring around it. Why did they add the silver ring to it? They added the silver ring to say, "This is not just any heart. This is not a symbol or a sign of just any human heart. This is a sign of a human heart that was blessed with purity". The white metal represents purity and the ring is around it to say this was the pure heart of Adam before he was deceived by Satan.

Heart symbolic of the social nature

So it represents our first father and he is the human concept that represents shared identity. All of us have this identity that is social, the social nature. The heart is symbolic, too, of the social nature. We love each other. Our heart registers each other. It tells us that our society of Muslims is ordered, really, for humanity, the same thing. It is ordered upon the social nature. When you look at the American flag and you see the red streaks. That is the social nature and the white streaks that is the conscious of the people. The conscious should be clear, pure and your passion should be social passion. Your love for people and your spirit for people, it should be coming from your heart. So there are red lines and white lines. Then you go up to the sky and and there is the dark blue of night and stars are in that dark blue area. The same way you read this you have to read these signs in the Qur'an, too. You have to read the Ka'bah the same way. You know their red doesn't represent just red. What value would a flag have to us if the red streak is just a red streak saying, "Oh, it is pretty?" Some of us are so ignorant that is the only way we see it, saying, "We've got a pretty flag, red, white and blue, with some pretty stars in it."

The Bible says, "The rejected stone became the corner". What was rejected? The common nature that Adam represents, the common human identity and nature were rejected. We all are identifying commonly, altogether, and there is a name for our nature among living things. What is the name for our nature? It is human nature. It is not dog nature, not reptile nature, not elephant nature. Human nature that is what we all have in common and nothing else has that but us humans.

The soul tends to dawn in the mind

The impulses (of man) are also called the fig tree and after Jesus Christ comes, he said, "You didn't have any food for me because G_d has formed my impulsive nature. So the fig tree of your world let it bear figs no more." Isn't that what it says? He cursed it to bear figs no more. Now, we don't see any fig tree that's cursed, that's not bearing figs. So that has nothing to do with those material things out there. It's all right inside of us. It's in the soul.

There's a tendency in the soul to dawn in the mind, in the intellect; and when it dawns upon impulse, oh all of a sudden intuition just brings so many things to your mind. It fills your mind up with lights, like the many seeds in a fig! Now, that's different from a figment. A figment means that this is off by itself. Figment in the heavens of our mind is like an asteroid or something going through space. But the bright order of stars is so many like the seeds in a fig. It says, "And your seeds shall be like the stars in the heavens; also, like the grains of sand on the seashore". But, they are going to rise up from there. Once you purify that material, clean it up and purify it, the next stage is going to shoot you up to the sky! The night sky is going to show you so many lights that you're not going to be able to count them.

The urge in Abraham's intellect

So, from the love for purity you rise to enlightenment. That's what it is saying. "Your seeds shall be as the sand on the seashore". You won't be able to count the grains of sand. So who is He talking to? He's talking to Father Abraham and Abraham is the man of rational faith. "By you being the leader of all people on the earth for rational faith, you're going to first bring those people who are pure of heart to you and your following shall be like the grains of sand on the seashore; so many you're not going to be able to count them".

But then the next progression is going to be for the intellect, because G_d is going to bring them to the intellect. If they become pure at heart they are not going to have to bring themselves into the intellect. G_d is going to bring their reasoning to burst into a bright galaxy and it's going to be in the rational mind. It's going to come from purity to the rational mind and your rational thoughts shall fill the heavens; and it is going to be so pure they're going to call it the saints. It's really beautiful!

It's talking about the urge in Abraham's intellect, that his urge stems from the purity of his heart and he was a man of great faith; great and unshakable faith. But, he respected logic and he respected the reasoning supported by logic so strongly that he never would separate his rational from his spiritual. He kept the two together until they became reconciled. He understood that one is not against the other. Both are given to man to carry man to the destiny. So he became a father, a leader for all mankind, for all people.

Letting them stay in the womb

However, he tended to believe that the spiritual wasn't as valuable for going to the end. He believed that for the goal that the community of people seek on the earth the spiritual was in the way. The spiritual was holding them back. But it was holding them back because it had hot reconciled itself with the rational. So when G_d told him to kill his son it pained him that he had to kill his son. That's the ignorant, spiritual masses. So it pained him that he had to kill him. You know he was a good man. He was a father to everybody. He loved everybody and he cared for the poor. And how was he caring for them? He was caring for them by letting them stay in the womb. Yes, that's how he was caring for them, by letting them stay in the womb. As long as you're in the womb you can be at peace.

But G_d said, "No, they can't stay in the womb. I want them all to come forth to My destiny that I planned for them". When Abraham understood that he said, "I've got to kill my own child?" It pained him greatly. Then, Allah said to him, "No, you don't have to kill him. Just kill that sheepish nature in him and feed that sheepish nature to the people. Let them be educated regarding their sheepish nature; that you don't take it to the extreme where you don't defend yourself and let the wolves come in and other things keep taking advantage of you." So he stood the sheep up in a man's clothing, in warrior's clothing.

The feeding is taken to the New Testament and to Jesus Christ. The feeding is not really killing something and then feeding it to something. No, the feeding is teaching. "Take this bread, symbolic of my body, the doctrine of the New Testament, the teachings of the New Testament. So how do you feed my sheep? You teach them of my knowledge that G_d gave to me as my body." Isn't that something, that a man sees his body as his education, as his knowledge, not as his physical flesh? From this we get the language, "Body of knowledge".

Science separate from religion

So Abraham kept them separate. He kept science separate from religion and he didn't feel that he was responsible for religion. He was a rational man, teacher, an educator. But then his mind led him to believe that in order to go further, keep moving forward with true knowledge, it was going to mean the death of the spiritual community. And he didn't want to see them left so far behind that they would become of no importance for the future of the real life on earth. So he thought that G_d was opening his eyes to tell him, "You can't carry them and much as you cherish this and have this sentimental attachment to the spiritual people, they just can't make it into the future. So you should make a sacrifice". He thought he should sacrifice them.

This is addressing what happened before in society. The social people were sacrificed to have the spiritual people advance and Abraham was of the mind that the spiritual life had to be sacrificed so we could have the social life the way it should be. So when the figure was rejected or transformed as a sheep that's the answer. The sheep are peaceful like a typical priestly society. The sheep are typical of those who want the life of peace and they like to be to themselves. They are close to each other. So the picture I have in mind of that spiritual order back there was a kind of order that existed before Prophet Muhammed came and led the people into community life and whatever and guided them to be responsible for the needs of community life.

'Eid means a recurring happiness and we have two 'Eids. The 'Eid al-Fitraa is the 'Eid celebrating the victory of human nature. 'Eid al-Adha is celebrating the victory of the intellect that is associated with Prophet Abraham, also pronounced Ibraheem. He led the world into the fulfillment of the needs or the appetites of the intellect, the human brain. He is the one who showed us the way to an ethical world, an ethical society, firstly, of believers but eventually to an ethical world; because the work of the believers will eventually triumph over the work of the unbelievers. We are not the only children of Abraham. The Jews are the children of Abraham. The Christians are the children of Abraham. I believe Abraham had many more children that we do not know about and they want an ethical world like we do. They want an ethical order.

Sacrifice of life

The tenth day of the Hajj is the Day of Sacrifice. On this day we sacrifice whatever we can afford. Poor people may sacrifice a chicken or something smaller that is halal, fit to eat. Those who have more money will sacrifice a cow or a sheep. The sheep is the symbol associated with Abraham because of his son, Ismail, being the son that he thought he should sacrifice. He saw in a vision that he should sacrifice him. But G_d showed him when he was about to sacrifice him, a sheep, a lamb, instead of Ismail.

So Abraham, the father, was shown in a vision by G_d a lamb, not his son, Ismail. He was to see the lamb. The lamb was to be slaughtered, not Ismail. But his son is symbolic of the lamb without spot or blemish, a lamb pure, untainted, unspoiled, by the world. That is symbolic also of Jesus Christ. As you know, he was called a lamb and before him we talk about Isma'il as the lamb. Muhammed, the Prophet, in his nature was also a lamb without spot or blemish before he was even called by G_d.

On the tenth day we sacrifice whatever we can afford to sacrifice but it is a sacrifice of life. It is a living thing that you are sacrificing and there was an ancient philosopher who said, "In man can be found all the creatures of the earth." So he said this long before people brought us the teachings on these things in religion. This is in myth or in Greek philosophy. We don't sacrifice something inferior or something offensive to good human nature or good human taste. You can't sacrifice a coon. It won't be accepted. What does sacrifice mean? It deceives us what is happening because it appears that you are getting rid of this thing, but you did not get rid of it. You made it tasty and then you consumed it. You put it in yourself. So it is symbolic of what is in us, but what is not quite ready for G_d. It is not quite good enough for G_d.

A sheep nature in a man is not quite good enough for G_d. The lamb goes up on the mountain and the lamb can stand on a little thin edge. It is sure footed and it has great balance. It is not the real lamb. It is symbolic of the social nature of the wise and pious people in religion, those who have the knowledge of not only spiritual sciences, but they have the knowledge of the spiritual sciences that helps us free the social life for its destiny that G_d wants for it. These are great, pious men of science and they are called the sheep in the scriptures. So these are great, pious men of science and they are called sheep. Ismail was going to be that kind of leader and Abraham was a rational man. He didn't like to have secrets and mysteries.

Abraham wanted liberal education

Abraham wanted liberal education for the people. He didn't want the knowledge to be held by people who were mystics who kept it secret for their elects. He wanted to break that order. So Abraham broke from that order and that is the meaning of slaying the lamb and feeding it to the multitudes. He broke from that order and gave the keys to their sciences to the multitudes. This is the one that G_d loves so much He said, "I will make you leader of all people" The Bible says, "You shall be a father of all the nations".

The sacrificing of the sheep or the lamb involves steps, not just cutting Let's begin with the first part of the process that brings it to the table and brings it to be ready for the guests to start eating. The first process is your handling of the animal to kill or slaughter it. You handle it with as much gentle care as possible. According to the way of the Prophet Muhammed's sunnah you make the knife very sharp so that the pain is not prolonged. It is very quick, cutting to have the least pain possible come to the victim. You sacrifice the sacrificial lamb and then the blood comes out. You want to drain as much of the blood as you possibly can and this is the blood of the lamb. Scripture says the blood is the life of that lamb. So actually you're draining that creature of its life. Its life is not going to be in it anymore. So you rejected its life. You don't want its life. You can't eat the blood. It is not halal.

So you rejected the life of the lamb. Now, you're eating its meat. Meat represents its teachings or doctrine, as the Bible says. And the blood was not fit to be taken directly. So you don't take the blood itself. You drink wine, representing the blood. The wine is not the biological life of that creature, but its talking about a human community, or human congregation. The wine is their spirit and the spirit of the sheep is sweet. The wine is sweet and the wine will lift your spirits and make your soul feel so good. So you now have transferred the reality from a sheep to a sheepish people and they are sheep-like because they think they're supposed to be that way. They think to please G_d they're supposed to be against violence, not have a rebellious spirit. They're supposed to be peaceful and accommodating.

So really what this is all about is not sacrificing people who are sheepish, but educating people who are sheepish; educating them in the knowledge of their own nature so they will remain peace loving people but will know when to stand up. You have to bring light into the dead matter. Abraham was destined to be a teacher for mankind and what was a problem for him was being a leader for the spiritual people who were sheepish. So G_d showed him how it doesn't mean you sacrifice your son. Do not sacrifice these people. They are your students and your student is your son. Don't sacrifice people, physically. Don't reject them and throw them away, but use their own nature as the way of educating them so that they will not just give themselves to pressures and other communities that will use them. Educate them. That is what we have to do. We have a lot of them but we're trying to educate them. Jesus Christ, peace be on him, he is the sheep, himself. But he is the enlightened sheep, so he speaks out in defense of the rest of the sheep. Jesus said, "As you have done to the least of them you have done it to me." It is beautiful.

Sheep references social community

So, Muhammed, the Prophet, was like Moses and Jesus is a sign pointing to Prophet Muhammed. His community is the community of Abraham and Abraham was a man of rational faith. So his community is not a spiritual community. Muhammed's community is a social community. Prophet Muhammed's community is not a spiritual community. That's not the description for it. Yes, we are a spiritual people. We have our spirituality. We have spiritual interests, etc., or spiritual life. But we, by description, are not a spiritual community. We are a social community.

And that's what's told in the sheep. Abraham's son is shown as a sheep. And a sheep only means or has reference only to a community that is strong in its social nature, constituted socially, in a very strong, strong way. That's all the sheep is symbolic of. That's the meaning for the sheep. Now, the predicament for the sheep in the world you can understand it. Until G_d makes the sheep, man (the sheep has to become man) that is, give him position, authority and rule in the world, the sheep's life is threatened and his situation in the world is very, very insecure.

World leaders fear nothing more than a development in obedient people to G_d that is social. They don't want you to have your social life; not in their social order. We have a democracy now that I think can accommodate other social orders in its social order. I do believe that. But the world, the governments of yesterday, they would not tolerate any other social orders. You could have your spiritual order, but not your social order; not in their government. So that's why there was so much fighting between the religious people and the worldly people; so many wars, religious wars they say. The world wouldn't tolerate you having your own community or your own social order. And that's what it's saying, that the destiny for the people of scripture is that they should have their own community life; their own social order. They are not to live in the social sciences or in the social order of the world. They're to establish their life upon the social order that G_d reveals.

Education supported by natural creation

So let us try to see our religion not only with our heart and with our sensitivities. But let us see our religion with our rational mind. Abraham, our second father, he is a sign of the excellence of the human brain and intellect. The Promised Land that is associated with this father of ours, it is education supported by natural creation, the sciences and all of the other beautiful things that come out of the search for better life through the nature of the material world, or the order of the material world. Scientists are born when they give themselves to this focus. The Qur'an inspired that focus in the early following of our Prophet Muhammed and in an amazingly short time universities, centers of higher learning, sprang up. People came from distant places to see those universities in Iraq, Africa, Morocco, and other places. They came to see the wonderful places where education was dawning afresh on this planet earth. Because of that the intellectuals of the West were aroused to devote themselves anew to the study of the creation and the development of the sciences.

3

Moses: The Liberator

Dear people of faith, history repeats itself. G_d blessed those rebellious, arguing followers of Moses to be led out of bondage into the Promised Land and they got out there and they sat down on him. So G_d said, according to the Bible, "This generation can't be used. You have to linger in the wilderness for forty years, until a new generation comes forward." Now you know all of Moses' people were not in that bunch. Moses had followers that were not like that. "So let them linger in the wilderness, we're going to Paradise. We're going to the Promised Land!"

$\mathcal{T}$here is a saying in the Qur'an, the holy book of the Muslims that says, "By the Fig and the Olive and Mt. Sinai and this town made safe, secured, surely We have created the human being in the best of molds." There was a time when there were no public schools. Public schools came late in the history of nations where, according to the law, you have to send your children to school. If you don't, you are subject to be put in jail, taken to court and locked up for not permitting your children to get an education.

I believe that the reference I just gave from our Holy Book has in it the importance of education. It is addressing the stages in the mind, the intellect; the stages of how the mind develops. The first is given in a picture of the fig but the Qur'an doesn't give any commentary on the fig. It leaves the commentary for the scholars. It leaves the commentary for the thinkers. When you think about the fig it is bigger than the olive and it has many seeds, whereas the olive has just one seed. So it goes from a product or a fruit that is easy to chew, the fig. You don't have to worry about a fig. Even if it is dry you don't have to worry about it. If you bite an olive and don't have any caution, you are going to break your dentures. Even a young person might hurt his teeth. If you bite down on that stone inside, it is hard. It is not like the fig that you can chew through. The olive has only one seed, but you must be careful eating it. You can't rush and eat it, like you do the fig. The fig has many seeds. It's like a burst of seeds. Think about the expression, "That's a figment of your imagination."

Fig represents common mind

The olive is in the Bible and it is also in the Qur'an. The Qur'an mentions the fig, first. The fig is kind of put down in the Bible, but here the Qur'an is picking the fig back up. It says: "By the Fig, by the Olive, by Mt. Sinai." Mt. Sinai is the mountain that Moses went up on and G_d spoke to him there. G_d gave him revelation on Mt. Sinai. Mt. Sinai is referring to ascending up, going higher up to G_d, getting communication from G_d and then coming back down. The third in this reference is Mt. Sinai, and the fourth reference is the town. The Qur'an says, "And this town made safe." How do you make the town safe? You make the town safe by respecting all the people. All of us have imagination, but all of us do not have olives. All of us can think and we have vivid imaginations, most of us. So respect the common mind. I think the fig is symbolic of the common mind. It is a metaphor representing the common mind and G_d is telling us to respect the common mind.

Olive represents the learned leaders

Then, respect those who are looking for a single thought or single interest. They are focused on one thing and those are the educated people. They focus on one thing and they stay focused on that until it becomes illuminated. Like oil, you can strike a match near it and get fire. So they focus on one thing so long, until it illuminates for them and then they get the insight. They get the knowledge and they pass it on. These are all stages.

Respect for everybody

The Qur'an says, "And the town made safe". It includes the town because we have to develop in the town. You can go up on the mountain and you can get all of that good knowledge and good insight. But if you don't come back down and live with people you will never know how to use it. Where do we learn how to communicate with one another? We learn it by living with one another. We live with one another and we learn how to communicate with one another. We live with one another, then we know how to apply our knowledge. It takes this social interaction to show us how to apply knowledge, where to put it and how to use it.

If we never have a chance to socialize or have social interaction, we will never truly become educated. To have light and not put it to use is no education. I am sure when Moses came down from the mountain he had a great light. But he had to come down and look at his people's circumstances and then see how he was to use that light that G_d gave him on the mountain, to see how to apply it; and he wasn't selfish.

This is the same Moses who is in the Bible and Qur'an. He is for both of us. He wasn't a selfish man saying, "I'm going to do this by myself." The first thing he did was to look around and see what resources he had. He said, "Okay, you doctors get together. You lawyers get together. You farmers get together. You musicians get together." Moses started organizing people according to their skills and abilities, etc. Then he gave them what G_d gave him from the mountain, and he charged all of them with responsibility to use it, apply it and make their lives conform to it. We can't do all of that. That is too much for us. We are not Moses. But what we can do is have respect for everybody.

Al-Islam begins with the promotion of good character and good character is respect for everything that deserves respect. A person of good character respects your property. You give him your key and say, "Here is my key. You can use my car to go to the store and pick up some groceries. You don't have a car." A person of good character will not abuse that trust. He will treat the car just like it belongs to him and even better. If he's such a person who doesn't care too much about a Rolls Royce, it could have been a wagon, but you trusted him with a Rolls Royce. So he's going to give it the respect that a Rolls Royce deserves, not the respect that a wagon deserves. So you have to be of good character to have healthy citizenship.

Moses went up the river to a kingdom

We did not get this religion easily. We got it the hard way, but so did the people of Moses. They got it the hard way, too. They were in bondage. They were under Pharaoh and Moses as a child, or baby, peace be upon him, was sent up the river or down the river. But he went up, because he went to a kingdom. He went to a great, great kingdom of the Pharaohs. He was sent there and he became one of the workers in the upper level of leadership for Pharaoh. G_d made him to know His calling eventually and when he separated from Pharaoh the trouble started for him and his people. They were already in bondage, not Moses, because he was sent where he could be free with Pharaoh. But once he rejected Pharaoh, then he was in the same situation with his people. And G_d guided him over a long period of time. He was guided and finally his people were delivered, freed from bondage and they were free to have their own life and their own establishment, their own culture, their own life, their own establishments.

Dear people of faith, history repeats itself. G_d blessed those rebellious, arguing followers of Moses to be led out of bondage into the Promised Land. They got out there and they sat down on him. So G_d said, according to the Bible, "This generation can't be used. You have to linger in the wilderness for forty years, until a new generation comes forward." Now you know all of Moses' people were not in that bunch. Moses had followers that were not like that. "So let them linger in the wilderness. We're going to Paradise. We're going to the Promised Land!"

Make connections again

The obligation on us to stand up on our own feet and to be responsible for our own families and for our own neighborhood, for the areas that we live in, is as much a holy obligation as saying prayers, as making Hajj (Pilgrimage), as witnessing that there is but one G_d. Yes, it is. Why? It is because we were once connected with G_d, Allah and many of us were connected who came over here as slaves. We were connected with the Qur'an and Muhammed and that was taken away from us. Our possessions, our holy, sacred possessions, were taken away from us and we were raised up as slaves and beaten down to the position of inferior people. Now, G_d wants to bring that back, to make the connections, again.

Their babies were innocent. Maybe they were guilty. Maybe they didn't keep the law. Maybe they didn't respect the Qur'an. Maybe they didn't respect the way of Muhammed, so they deserved what was done to them. But what about their children, their babies? We are innocent and G_d will save the innocent. He will destroy the whole universe to save the innocent. So don't think I don't have power. I have the power of the prophets, because what I'm doing is the work of the prophets; and G_d started this, not me.

In our Holy Book, G_d says, "Oh you who have faith, be not like those who worked to harm the works of Moses. However, G_d strengthened him (meaning Moses) in righteousness against what they uttered, and he was honorable in G_d's presence". Here is G_d asking all of us to be not like those who worked to harm Moses. Moses in his flesh? No, they worked to make him not worthy of the high honor that G_d had created him for and he was earning as a prophet of G_d. It was to take away that honor and to attribute falsehood and sin and weakness to the man, to spoil his beautiful character in the eyes of the people, so they would be freer as followers of his to give themselves also to sin. The ones who do work like that are really very close to the Satan, himself. They work very close as supporters of the Shaitan, the Satan, himself.

Qur'an's role to serve as imam

The Qur'an says, "It is Allah Who teaches you"; teaches you plural, not singular. It can't be speaking to the Prophet. It is obvious that He spoke to the Prophet. Allah communicated to us through the Prophet. But He says it is Allah who teaches you. So that means, yes, the Prophet teaches you, but if you deserve it G_d will teach you, Himself, if the time deserves it. And all the time it is G_d who is teaching you, because the Qur'an is His word to all of us. And if you study sincerely you are going to be educated in the Qur'an without a teacher. All of us get guidance and all of us get better educated in al-Islam by reading and studying the Qur'an.

The Qur'an, based upon what G_d says of Moses and his people, its role is also to serve as our imam. It says he revealed the book as an imam to the people of Moses. That is to tell us our book, too, is a man like unto Moses. So, our Qur'an, too, is revealed to us to be our imam. You see the movement of al-Islam in the prophet is the liberation of mankind, all people. But what has prevented the people from being awakened to their best nature and the course they could take to freedom? It is religious leaders who keep the whole pot and give the people a little broth. That has been the problem.

So the Qur'an and Muhammed, the Prophet, come to make it available to everybody; and they don't have to come through anybody; no intercessor, no mediator, no one who mediates between G_d and you and no priesthood. That means our religion doesn't depend on religious or spiritual leaders to keep it in the public. Men and women are obligated to follow the sunnah of our Prophet where no one leads the other. You are to perform it independently, on your own. All of that points to the order that we need for mankind on earth to get rid of all forms of slavery. So Prophet Muhammed is to be seen as a liberator, a teacher who teaches universality, universals and situates us to get the maximum benefit from academic studies, or interest, or education.

The knot in Moses' tongue

Muhammed is called a man like Moses. What is the understanding that we're to get from that statement in Qur'an, that Muhammed is the one that's promised to the people that would be raised up among the men, the common men, the brethren, it's translated; a man like Moses? What are we to understand from that? Moses was a man who was not educated. How do we know that? He had to have the help of Aaron, his brother, to communicate. G_d gave him his brother Aaron as a Prophet, too. Aaron was made a prophet by G_d. He gave him his brother Aaron as a helper to him, to help him communicate. Why? It was because his tongue had a knot in it. What is to be understood by a knot in his tongue? It means that he was not of educated language. He was not of eloquent speech, etc. He was not an educated man. That was the knot in his tongue.

Moses was not educated by his people. He couldn't have been educated by his people, because he was sent from his people as an infant upon the river in a little basket that was made to keep out the water and sealed with tar. He was put upon the river and sailed down the river. It was Pharoah's wife, according to scripture and history, who took him from the water and took him into their home. Now you say, "Well, he went into the home of the big lady of the Egyptian empire," if we want to call it empire. I don't know whether they would call it empire in that time, but we can say empire. So, you would think that he was educated by the Egyptians. Look how many of us have been taken into the empire of the United States of America and never learned a dammed thing! Excuse my language, please! But we never learned a dammed thing and we were taken right into the house of the big people. So don't think he had to be educated because he was taken into the house. They took him into the house for special services, just like they took us into the house for special services but didn't educate us properly.

So he was not educated properly and when his own people told him that he was going to be their liberator, he was surprised. He couldn't understand it. He didn't think he was qualified to be their liberator and he didn't really understand until G_d, Himself, called him. When G_d spoke to him he was searching because he didn't like his people suffering under the Egyptians. So he got himself in trouble with the Egyptians. He was searching for understanding and he told his wife, "I think I see a fire at the foot of the mountain. I'm going there. Perhaps I will be able to bring something to warm us with from the fire." He went to the mountain and when he got there both scriptures, Bible and Qur'an, say G_d spoke to him and told him that he was on sacred ground; to take off his shoes. From that time he became aware. G_d began to teach him. G_d became his Teacher.

You know there's something about his relationship with his brother, Aaron (peace be upon the prophets), that we should understand, too. Though Aaron did a job, he did that job in subordination to Moses. He was not over Moses. He didn't tell Moses, "Okay, Moses, now I have to do my job." Moses told him, "Now, you have to do your job." So, actually, the great knowledge was given to Moses. Aaron threw down the rod according to scripture and his rod defeated the tricks of the magicians of Pharaoh, who also threw down rods which appeared to be serpents, snakes, living snakes, moving about. Moses had been given this knowledge, but it was Aaron who was told to do the job. Do you follow? Those of you who have studied this, do you recall this? Yes, it was Aaron who did the job of throwing the rod down, but it was Moses who had been given the knowledge.

"What's that in your hand, Moses?"

G_d asked him, "Moses, what is that you have in your hand?" He said, "This is my staff, my rod." He said, "What do you do with that?" He said, "I walk with it and I beat brush back to open the path for me to walk." So G_d said, "Throw it from you." And when he threw it from him, it turned into a big snake and Moses became afraid and withdrew, got back from it. And G_d said, "Now take it into your hands again (He told him how to take it) and it will become as it was before, your staff, your rod." So G_d had already shown Moses the great science or the great mystery of the staff, of the rod. Therefore Aaron wasn't doing something that Moses had no knowledge of. But he just had the language. He could speak the language that was understood by the Egyptians and that would impress the Egyptians; whereas, Moses could not speak to them clearly. His tongue was tied. He had a knot in his tongue.

G_d is man's first teacher

Both of these prophets are signs of the great proof that G_d gives. What is that proof? It is proof that He, G_d, taught man. G_d Who created the universe is man's teacher. How am I taught by my teacher in the school, in the classroom? My teacher communicates to me from her or his mind what they have gotten and my teacher is assisted with textbooks, blackboards, writing pens or pencils, chalk and all of these things. That's how I'm taught by my teacher. G_d says He taught man the use of the pen (Qur'an). Now do we accept that or not? If G_d says He taught man the use of the pen, we know the oldest education exists for us in the form of ancient writings. We call it print, now. It comes in print or in writing and G_d says He is the one Who taught the man the use of the pen. And G_d also proved it. He said it and He proved it; that all knowledge came from G_d and G_d is the Teacher, the First Teacher.

The prophets were big in their times. Yes, Noah was big in his time, biggest man on earth in his time. Moses was the biggest man on earth in his time. But in the day of Muhammed they become small, because Muhammed's day does not exalt Muhammed. It exalts the Word of G_d, praise be to Allah. Moses, he had a very difficult time with his people. They were really forced into the circumstances they were in. They didn't all want to be with Moses. Circumstances forced them to be with Moses and I'm not comparing us now. There's a strong comparison. But I'm comparing Moses, the Prophet and Muhammed, the Prophet. Moses had a difficult time with his people. They were suspicious of him. They didn't trust that this man knows what he's doing and why didn't they trust him? It was for more than one reason. The most important reason was that he was not produced by powers or influences that they knew and understood. So when he was away from them up in the mountain trying to get an audience with G_d he stayed so long they ran out of patience and they elected Moses' brother, Aaron, to be the leader. They made Aaron their leader in the absence of Moses and then gave suggestions to Aaron and Aaron followed their suggestions. And they started building the golden calf, false god, deity, in the absence of Moses.

A new societal order

Now here comes Muhammed, a man like Moses. Here is Muhammed coming, the last prophet, a man like Moses. How is he like Moses? Moses was put in a situation to be responsible for giving a new societal order to a people that had to exodus from one society into a desert where there was no society. So Moses had the job or mission of making a world for a people who had been put out of a world. They were put out of the world of Egypt into the desert and Moses was their leader. They had to trust him to guide them back to another societal order or another world order. Here is Muhammed in the world of paganism, idol worship, and he's given a mission by G_d to lead people out of the world of paganism into a new world order. Here's a man missioned to lead a people into a community, to form a community all over. Form a community means, form another societal order or another world order. That's what Islam is. It's a world order, a global order, an international community. In that respect they are men alike in their mission, Moses and Muhammed. But that's not all.

A man like Moses

Why did people argue with Moses? "He doesn't have credentials like Aaron. He's not articulate like Aaron. He does not have the tongue of the professional, like Aaron. This Moses was not with us. We didn't go to school with him. He was floated down the river as a baby and Pharaoh took him in. He had no education from us. Pharaoh made him a soldier and one to oversee the building construction. He's not trained in this language. What kind of man is this we're following, claiming he's something?" But Allah always gives such men in their loneliest hours some persons that believe in them. Moses had them. Muhammed had them. His wife, Khadijah, she believed in him and behind him another and another. G_d always blesses some few persons to believe in people like this in their most lonely hour.

He (Muhammed) was a man like Moses in that he was not educated by the world. The world didn't teach him. He didn't get his education, knowledge, from the world. The point is there's a reason for Moses having all that difficulty he had with his people and Muhammed not having all that difficulty. Muhammed's difficulty was with the idolatrous people, the pagan idol worshipers. He didn't have a whole lot of difficulty with his own people. His own people gave him allegiance and fought so strongly with him that they welcomed death for the glory of the mission of Islam. They told the enemy, "Are you ready to fight? Are you sure?" They said, "Let it be known that you're meeting a people in battle that love death more than you love life". That was something to shake a man's nerve. I would have had some second thoughts if I were on the other side. I'd say, "Maybe this is not the day for me to go out". I would have been looking for a way to disappear from the ranks.

Moses killed a man and that seems to be the big mark against Moses in scripture; a mark that stayed with him even after Muhammed. David killed many men. Solomon killed many men. Now why is it a special thing with Moses for killing one man? This one man was the enemy of his people and was threatening the life of one of his own people. What's the big deal that Moses killed a man?

As though he killed humanity

Shouldn't you want to know? It's not what you see, or what you're looking at. You're looking at Moses killing an Egyptian because that Egyptian was threatening a Hebrew. That's what you're looking at and Moses acting in anger killed that man. You have to understand that in light of the community aspirations or the national aspirations of the people called Hebrews, Jews, or Israelites. Moses killed a man, meaning Moses up to that point in his life was working for Jews, Hebrews, or Israelites, not for humanity. So here's an attack upon the Egyptians. Killing that Egyptian was as though he killed humanity. His killing the Egyptian was killing human kind to bring them closer to the mission of addressing the need to advance humanity forward to where G_d wants humanity to go. They had such a burden and were so difficult to deal with that their own leaders were drawn into that interest.

The Moses that killed this Egyptian was not the Moses that had gone up Mt. Sinai. This is the Moses who was told by some of his people that, "You are to be our deliverer". G_d hadn't told him that. It was his people that told him, "You are to be our deliverer", to get him out of Pharaoh's house to fight for their cause. So he was the man that struck the Egyptian and killed him.

Muhammed, the Prophet, before G_d called him, he went into the mountain, too, the mountain of the light. Before G_d called Muhammed, Muhammed had not done anything to make any citizen in the land where he lived suspect that he had any spot or blemish. They saw him without spot or blemish. He had not killed anybody over anything. His interest in his people was not nationalistic. He had no nationalist interests in his people. He mourned the condition of his people before Allah called him, before he went up in the mountain. He saw their condition as being pitiful and he was searching for certain ways to bring assistance to them to take them out of their condition.

A great human life

Muhammed was looking at Jahiliyyah, ignorant age Arabia. But Muhammed had traveled outside of Arabia as a businessman working for Lady Khadijah, doing trade. He had been to Syria, to other places, gone outside of Saudi Arabia and he had met people from different lands in trade. Muhammed was not ignorant of what the world looked like at that time. He knew what the world looked like at that time. So Muhammed was weeping, not as some Arabs will tell you. He wasn't just weeping the condition of the bad state of the Arabs. He was weeping for the bad social, community state of humanity at that time and his interest was not, I repeat, in bringing Arabs to have a great nation. His interest was in bringing his fellow citizens to have a great human life. That was his interest, just to have a great human life. So he was not about killing any man. He was about saving mankind and that's why G_d chose him and didn't have to undo him to do him, like he had to undo Moses to do Moses.

"What is that you have in your hand, Moses? That isn't going to work here unless I can change it. Moses, take off your shoes". His shoes were not acceptable. Where he was standing shoes weren't acceptable and his staff that he leaned upon and used to beat the brush, to get through the thicket, was not acceptable; not as it was. But Muhammed didn't have anything that was not acceptable. "Oh you and your mantle arise and warn". It didn't say, "Oh you and your mantle what are you wearing there? The only problem you have is you need what I have; and don't worry. We are going to enrich you to the point where you will have no more wants". Praises be to G_d. "There's nothing wrong with your heart, but we're going to expand your breast for a weighty word". That's G_d talking in the Qur'an.

The people of Moses came from a land that had big achievements in the visible world. Their achievements were visible; that is, their achievements were physical and material, not just spiritual. They had managed very strong spiritual achievements, the ancient Egyptians, under that particular pharaoh and other pharaohs, too. The people of Moses were used to seeing things just where nobody had to have a plan to get bread. Egypt had plenty of bread. Nobody had a plan to have comforts. Egypt had plenty of comforts. But here you are leaving Egypt going out on your own and it is going to require faith, good deeds, patience and a commitment to truth and reality. While Moses was up there they lost faith in him and patience. They couldn't keep patience. He was up in the mountain seeking G_d for light and understanding for them that would benefit the society. But they couldn't have patience with him.

A society of wisdom

So they showed haste. "We want it quick. He's up there. He's a holy man. We don't have time for that kind of leader. Aaron, you know how to direct this thing. Build, make for us a golden calf. We want a society of wisdom. We don't need this special guidance that he's looking for. We want a society of wisdom like Egypt has. So make us a society of wisdom and do it quickly", because the golden calf was a young calf. The language says it was very youthful and quick. In Arabic, it is, "Ajlan", from "ajala", from which we get the word, "to hasten, go fast".

It did not say, "Golden Cow". It said, a "Golden Calf". Calf is the baby, young, ready to rip and run. So it is not talking about what you know. What do we have? What kind of society have we been brought to? This was not like it was when I was a boy. Now, we have a very fast-paced society, don't we? And we have fast food. Everything is fast. They want it just like that. And we have more corruption than we ever dreamed could come into our lives. So these things are not pictures of something back there. They are pictures of what is going to happen as man multiplies and grows in wealth and comforts. So it is future oriented. The language is future oriented, although this back there was nothing like what the language points to; because all the time that this is going on G_d's promise is with the people. Actually, the promise

He made the first time was with the first man, Adam, when He told him, "All this is for you. I made it to yield its benefits to you." When He told Adam that, it was the first promise. Then, came His promise to Abraham, because man went out on his own and made the world so difficult for a righteous person to live in.

Language of secret religion

So then He makes His promise to Abraham, the second father, before He revealed to Moses. Moses is doing his part of the book, his scripture. He's living his part of the scripture. His people, they are living that part of the scripture. But at the same time, the promise is still hanging over their heads; G_d's promise. They wanted to get out of Egypt and have independence so they could live like the Egyptians lived. So, "We're not interested in this conversation that you want to have with your G_d. We know how to get over. We want to get over like Egypt got over. Aaron can you help us?" And he could. That is why G_d gave Moses, Aaron, because he could read the wisdom of the Pharaoh or of ancient Egypt. That is why G_d gave him to Moses as an assistant or as a helper, so that when he had to deal with or meet the challenge of Pharaoh's high priests and those who were high in the secret or hidden knowledge, he had Aaron to help him. Like Prophet Muhammed, Moses couldn't read scripture. He could not read the language of secret religion or wisdom. They said, "Can you make us a golden calf?" Now, if they asked a question they knew the wisdom existed. They were not an ignorant society for they knew that he was the most advanced in that skill. That is why they asked him to do it. Then what he says to them in reply says exactly what I just said. He said, "Give me your earrings," meaning give me the wisdom you hear that 'rings' a bell for you. You have a lot of wisdom here in this gathering or in this faithless community". They were a people of no faith.

Moses a dual figure

Two arrows fired from one bow going parallel to the target is referenced in the story (in Qur'an) of the search of Moses and the wise man, where the wise man says, "We have to part ways. The fish went away, sped away, as though in a channel and it is behind us now. We missed it". That is to say Moses did not experience this. Moses had not experienced this. His will had not come into perfect harmony in agreement with G_d's will and purpose; not yet. He did not know the purpose. That is why the wise man was taking him on a journey to teach him wisdom. He did not know the purpose. If I would tell you that there is no Aaron, that Prophet Aaron is our brother outside of Moses' own soul and existence, would you believe it? Well, I just told you. Moses is a dual figure. Would he be stupid and Pharaoh had him building for him? He was a builder, a professional. It's like me asking you, "Prophet Muhammed couldn't read and he is doing business, going to Syria and other countries?"

Now they are on two different levels, not like John and Jesus. Prophet John and Prophet Jesus, they are on the same level in the Ascension. But Moses and Aaron are on two different levels. Aaron was on the fifth and Moses was on the sixth level. So Moses' mission is six, sixth level, the social mission and his brother is on the fifth level, meaning he is on the rational level. The Children of Israel were strongly rational. They questioned spiritual things and they were slow to accept spiritual knowledge. The wanted only the rational. They wanted the rational basis. "Show me the rational side of this". So Aaron was their leader.

Moses was up in the mountain. They did not want him, anyway. So they said, "Aaron, make a Golden Calf. You know how to put this wisdom together. Make that Golden Calf." He said, "Give me your golden earrings". He said, "Let us do this thing. Give me your golden earrings. I will be your leader. I will put it all together for you." So he got their wives' earrings and put them all together and formed the Golden Calf. When Moses came down he snatched him by his beard for that.

Beard is mature knowledge

The beard is your mature knowledge, your wisdom, what you get in older years; and it is the knowledge that communicates. It communicates to the listener. The beard just goes up and down. The mustache is not going up and down. It looks like the mouth is opening and closing, but it is nothing but the lower jaw going up and down. The upper one is standing still in the heavens. The signs of G_d are everywhere in the world as well as in man. This is the Qur'an, the scripture. So the beard is symbolic of wisdom. And the wisdom that comes to man, most of the time it is in his late years and he communicates it to others. So Aaron pleaded, "Do not seize me by my beard!"

One person in a person

Moses asked G_d to untie the knot in his tongue. That is the same as saying "Give me a brother as a helper"; which means that he himself was not able to use the rational in the spiritual mission. It was too strange for him. So he is asking for a brother to do that. What it is saying is that this spiritual counterpart is in his own nature, in his own body, in his own spirituality, in himself, but as his brother. Now this language that shows more than one person in a person is all through scripture. When Jesus took his disciples up on the mountain to show them himself, it is called the Transfiguration. He showed them Moses and Elijah together in one light and I am saying that he was showing them, himself, Jesus Christ. So what is he saying about himself? He is saying that, "I am two in one. I am the light of Moses and I am the light of Elijah. Both have come together in me". So Moses and Aaron in the Ascension should be seen in the same way and he did not say that Moses was the same type as Elijah.

Aaron becomes Moses

So Moses and Aaron were not the same height, either. One was five feet and the other was six. But they both were in the same Ascension. They were in the same light beam going up to G_d; a proof that I am right. There are many proofs. I gave you some proofs, already. In the Bible Aaron throws the rod for Moses in the contests with the high priests. In the Qur'an it's the same. But read the whole Qur'an. In another place Moses throws the rod by himself. There is no Aaron with him. The Holy Qur'an also has Moses throwing the rod, not somebody else, not Aaron. So how is he able to throw the rod at this point? It is because Aaron has now become Moses. There is no more two, It is only Moses. The light of Aaron has merged and disappeared in the light of Moses and come into one beam in him. The man is much wiser, now. What it is saying is that, yes, he needed help in the early stages of his life. But eventually G_d educated Moses. He did not need Aaron. He threw the rod by himself.

Wise man also in Moses

Now it seems like it is one occasion, a big occasion where they meet. No, this challenge is all the time. It's all through the life of Moses. Pharaoh, his witchcraft producers, they are following him. So he has to keep throwing the rod. He has to keep manifesting his superior knowledge of their culture. That is what the rod is. G_d asked him, "What is that? What do you do with that?" He said, "Oh, I use it to support me when I am walking and I use it to beat back the bush from the path". This shows he had knowledge of the culture. We have to meet the challenge all of the time, too. We have to meet the challenge of darkness, superstition and witchcraft all the time and beat back the darkness, just as Moses did.

In the Qur'an, the wise man Moses had to follow when he found the junction of the two seas after retracing his steps is also in Moses. But Moses could not keep company with his own light of wisdom. He could only go so far and he would lose it. He would lose the ability to keep up with it. Before he knew anything he would have to say, "I missed something."

Everything an expression of soul

Really, the place for clarity is the soul. G_d created the soul, nobody else did; the original soul. So it seems as though we are in the world when we are reading Qur'an and reading history. That is true. But the real focus for what is going on, all the history, wars and everything is the human soul. It is as a looking glass in which you see all of these things. I don't know if it is called a looking glass. It is more precisely called a crystal ball. It is as a crystal ball in which we see the whole world in its stages and what is going on. And really you cannot see it until you first see the order of the soul or the nature of the soul. When you see the nature of the human soul, then, you can understand what is going on in the world. This is philosophy. But everything we have in this world, buildings and everything, I don't care how big or how small the station, mission, or program going out in space looking for possible life out there, everything is an expression of the soul.

Woman as metaphor

The soul asked for that and if man had not mated with woman and had children by her he would be still sitting up under a tree whistling *Dixie,* or smoking in the wilderness, nothing created. But when they mate, then the woman reproduces for the man and reproducing for him makes him more serious, gives him something to work for, a future; gives him a future to work for and gives him a bigger interest. So now he needs more, so he begins to seek more. And she is like a metaphor, or a sign of the original soul. From one soul He made two and what is the grammatical gender for the soul? It is feminine, not masculine. From one He made two, which means the order and nature of the soul is personified by the woman more than by the man. But when he engages her to produce or have his future with her, then her nature covers his nature, though his nature still leads her nature. He is the leader, but her nature covers his nature. When I say cover I mean influence and he becomes like her in his soul. He was not even aware of his soul before. But now she has made him aware of his soul. And she has made him have a sensitive soul. So that is feminine. She has made him a sensitive soul. So they become two and then G_d reproduces from them all the men and women on earth.

The soul keeps making requisitions

So it is the soul that begins the building of man's world. The soul begins expressing itself, "I want a building. I want a road." That is the soul asking for that before the mind asks for it. So when G_d says in the scripture, "To have comfort in her or in it", that is the soul. The soul is what is going to comfort. It wants peace. It wants comfort. And we think it stops. It never stops. It keeps requesting. It keeps making requisitions, "Put me up a road. Put me up a city." That is that woman, isn't it? Now when trouble comes in she looks to the man, "Put out those fires, man! Put out those fires! What is wrong with you? You're going to let everything burn up! You are going to let our whole investment, all of it, burn up!" He made the man and he was lonesome, alone, and G_d did not like that the man should be lonesome or alone. So He made for him a mate. Now, before He made for him a mate what had he done? He had done nothing. He was not asleep either, unless he was sleepwalking.

4

Jesus Christ: The Word and Spirit from G_d

The Bible speaks of Jesus Christ as a word and it says he was existing before the foundations of the world. That is to be understood in several ways. But one clear way is that G_d is saying that the world of mankind, the world we live in, it should conform to the plan of G_d and G_d's plan is for the ideal human being. It is not for every human being. It is only for the ideal human being. The ideal human being is man is his created excellence, the best moral life and the best rational life with all of the talents and possibilities for him in a real world. Jesus Christ is a sign of that and Muhammed, the Prophet, is the proof of that; not just a sign.

 Jesus Christ does not represent the only one who comes to tell the world, "Stop doing wrong. Stop mistreating the weak people. Start loving each other. Start helping the little guy. Come to the rescue of the weak and the suffering people." That's not the only Jesus. In fact, that Jesus is not a big deal, because we have those people all of the time in society, women and men who love to do good. And if they see wrong they want to tell you, "Don't do that. Don't be like that. Help that person. Don't treat him like that". They will stop what they are doing and come away from what they are doing. Maybe they were going to an important meeting or something. They will actually stop, just like the Good Samaritan. In fact, that speaks more to support what I'm saying than anything I can say to you.

 Jesus pointed to a man who was already doing what he should be doing. He said the rabbis, meaning the religious leaders, all had walked down that same road and there was a man lying in the road suffering. They just walked around him and it says some walked on the other side of the street, or on the other side of the road so they wouldn't be bothered, wouldn't have their conscience bothered by him. Some didn't have a conscience at all. They would stay on the same side of the road, walk right by him and do nothing for him and he's suffering in the road. Jesus Christ said along came the Good Samaritan. The Good Samaritan came and had compassion on him.

 The word Samaritan is from the word, Samar, the place called Samar. He was named after a place, a city, or an area; like you would say, "Along came the Chicagoan." That is how Jesus Christ was speaking. It means a person who came from another town. He saw him, had compassion on him and he took him and gave him help. He had to keep going because he (the Samaritan) had a destiny. He had a job, too. He went and found somebody. He went to a rescue place and he said, "Take care of this man and when I return I will pay you." This is really deep. What is this saying?

A man from Samar

First, it is saying that world that Jesus Christ came into it was unconscious, filled with people who had lost their original, pure and innocent moral sensitivities and they were just seeing suffering and passing by with no attention to it at all. Here comes this man from Samar, a different area. He comes through their area and has compassion on the suffering person in the road. That is what it is saying on the surface. But what is it also saying, because it says he promised that he was coming back? It is saying that same nature, that same moral make up, is in Jesus Christ. But he's using another figure to point to something that is in him. He is teaching and using another figure, but he is the one teaching. He is the one who is trying to change things, but he points to another figure. Goodness is not yours. It is put in you from G_d.

He is also saying something that will miss most of the educated in religion. He is saying your goodness is not originally your goodness. Your goodness is divine goodness. It was put in you from G_d. So he can guarantee that you're going to get help because it is not him alone who is doing this. He is an instrument. The Good Samaritan is the instrument of G_d. The Islamic teachings or sciences say the whole human family, with all of our abilities and all of our tools, are like nothing but one hand of G_d. G_d has one hand doing things and the whole human is race is nothing but like one hand. It says He has another hand that is taking care of the non-human creation, stars, planets, earth and all the material inanimate and animate, living things. He is taking care of all of that with one hand and He is taking care of human life and human affairs with His other hand.

You are acting just as His hand. All of us together represent nothing but His one hand. Isn't that something? It is a description given in a metaphor, using pictures to teach us, because G_d has no hands like we have. If you put all human beings together they don't look like that hand. They look like millions of human beings. But that is G_d's hand according to that teaching, which is to tell us that just like we use one hand G_d uses the whole human family, all human beings just like we use one hand. And that would be our right hand, because human beings are building things and doing delicate work, healing, operating, performing surgery. So, that must be His right hand. But look at what G_d says in another place in the scripture. He says to Satan, "Why do you not accept My special human that I made with My two Hands".

Allah's two hands

In one place He says all of the human world is just like His one hand. But in another place He says when He was making His certain special human being He used both of His hands; both the inanimate, the natural world and conscious human life. He used both, the conscious human life and the inanimate world, all of the natural world. He brought them together and reconciled their purpose in the mind of His special creature; so that the human being would use this creation as it should be used to benefit all human beings. It is wonderful. Whatever I say I'm not speaking for myself. I'm speaking from my knowledge of Qur'an, Bible and everything.

So Jesus, in the Bible, is the second Adam and he's the son of man. He's the son of Adam, but not directly. He didn't have a direct father. But by genealogy in the Bible you trace his existence back to Adam. It's called the genealogy of Jesus Christ. So he's the son of man and the son of Mary. He's the son of man by what reasoning? That Adam was his mother's father and also his father. That's why Muhammed, when he greeted the ones in the Ascension (the Miraj), he greeted Adam, "As Salaam Alaikum, my father Adam," to say that, "Yes, I'm from Adam. I'm descended from Adam". And G_d says in Qur'an, "No one dies or is resurrected accept on the pattern of Adam". It means on his life form, that he was a social man of the human race and we all are social. That social life is expressed as political life and whatever else, but we are originally and essentially social beings and the ummah (community) is a social community. That's why we say brothers and sisters.

Thought and recall

The scripture says they betrayed Jesus Christ for thirty pieces of silver and Joseph was sold for twenty pieces of silver. So here is Joseph representing one orientation in the mind or in the mental make-up of the person who is serving or striving for something. For Joseph it represents moral nature. His rational mind was moral. He did not have a rational mind that was secular. He was a perfect man in his moral nature; Jesus Christ, too. But Joseph typifies or represents that; whereas, Jesus Christ represents the spirit.

The spirit has three. My rational mind has two, essentially, thought and reflection, or thought and memory, thought and questioning, thought and examining, thought and rethinking. That is the mind. That is the nature of everybody's mind, thought and recall. Joseph was not like the average person who just thinks for whatever situation. Whatever the Prophet Joseph did or thought it was governed by righteousness or moral conscience. He refused to do wrong even when it would help him a lot, personally, to do wrong. If he had satisfied the big lady, the wife of the ruler who wanted him for her man, he could have gotten a lot because she was the big boss's wife. He could have gotten a lot from her but he refused her. And he refused those ladies under her who wanted him, too. He was accused by the lady of being forward with her and he was saved by his shirt that was torn from behind. It showed that the lady who wanted him was holding him. So that was the proof that he was innocent.

Jesus Christ is spirit and spirit comes naturally before it reaches the conscious. Its nature for us is just to be good, to be innocent, to not to want to do wrong. So the spirit is in our body; that is, in the body; the spirit is good in the body. Then the spirit comes to the mind. Flesh, mind, these are the stages. The baby is born flesh. The baby becomes conscious, now his spirit is in his mind or expressed from his mind, not only from is body. That is two. And we just mentioned Joseph, Yusuf, in Arabic, being typical of the mind, thought and reflection. That is the second.

The third with Jesus is purpose

So he (Jesus Christ) is guided by the Spirit of G_d or the Will of G_d. So this third dimension, for want of a better expression, is purpose. How do we know this? He said, "I have to be about my father's business." This is the Gospel, the New Testament. That means he has to do what G_d ordered him to do. That is exactly what he meant, saying "G_d has given me a job. I have to do what G_d gave me to do." This is what he said. So he was saying that his purpose in the world was to do what G_d ordered him to do, or what G_d had assigned him to do; that his purpose was to do that; when G_d moves us or when G_d inspires us. And he himself represents, now, not the rational life. Jesus Christ, himself, represents the spiritual life. We know this from scripture, from the New Testament and also from the Qur'an. Jesus Christ represents the spiritual life, not the brain with its intuitive powers, like Joseph, Yusuf. He represents the spirit and the spirit in him is the spirit to take him to his purpose. Where does that spirit come from? It comes from him struggling to obey G_d. So his spirit becomes the spirit of obedience to G_d and G_d will protect that spirit.

"Don't prepare any notes"

If you give your spirit to G_d in obedience to Him, G_d, Himself, protects that spirit. He assists that spirit. G_d, Himself, will assist that spirit. You don't know all of the time how you will handle a situation. If you are in that disposition, if that is your makeup, you trust G_d. Another way of seeing this is to look at what Jesus told his disciples. He said, "Don't prepare any notes. Don't prepare any speeches." He said, "Just go and when you get there the spirit will speak through you".

According to the Gospel, this is what he told his disciples. Not only does he represent that, but he was a teacher who was promoting that kind of trust in people. Trust G_d. You don't know. We don't know. He was their teacher saying, "I can't tell you everything." And he said that. He said, "I speak to you now in parables (proverbs)", meaning, "I can't explain all of this to you. But nevertheless, I will return and speak to you in plain language. Now you are speaking to me in parables. You're my teacher. What am I going to do? You are telling me to go to this country and speak to the people there. What am I going to do? Trust the spirit". That is what he told them. "Don't prepare anything. Just go there and G_d will speak through you. The Holy Spirit will speak through you".

That is what he told them. That is how he taught. What does that have to do with thirty? He is conscious of obedience to G_d. He's conscious of giving his spirit in obedience to G_d. The spirit represents the third, body, mind and spirit. Someone may ask, "Is that for us children, also" Yes. When you were a baby you were careful to listen to your mama and your daddy. You get up a little older and you start giving them the deaf ear and pretty soon you're acting on spirit. So the flesh was born innocent. Your mind was the second dimension. Your mind was turned on and your mind was, at first, obedient. Then, you gave up conscious effort to follow your mama and daddy or whoever you should be following. You gave up conscious effort and you gave your behavior to the world, to your friends and to the world. Now you're not thinking about the right and wrong of things, or whether you should go home now or stay out a little later. You're following your spirit. You have a spirit to stay out all night.

Man is created to be dominated by spirit

Everybody moves in those three dimensions. That is how they go. Your first dimension is your body, the rule of your body; then the rule of your mind and then your spirit. If you don't discipline your mind for G_d's sake, your spirit takes over. And if your spirit is not under G_d, the spirit of G_d, you go astray. You become self-destructive, destructive to others and other things. Eventually, your spirit destroys you. So, man is created to be dominated by spirit, because none of us can guarantee the society that our body will never do wrong. And none of us can guarantee the society that our mind will never do wrong; none of us, no matter how much you are educated. There are Ph. D's who go to jail for petty crimes, for shop lifting. There are Ph. D's who can't live a decent life because they have become alcoholics or drug addicts. So there is no guarantee that you're going to be saved by your body or by your mind. There is no guarantee that you're going to be saved by your spirit unless you give your spirit to G_d like Jesus Christ did, like Muhammed did and like all of G_d's servants did. If you give your spirit to G_d in obedience to Him, now you're really saved. You're saved from the limits of your own mind or the weaknesses of your own mind. You're saved from your body and your mind and your spirit that would be loose on its own, if you bring your spirit under G_d.

Man mature in his spirit is superman

Actually, it is the spiritual dimension that is the most important. A man who has become mature in his spirituality or in his spirit he is superman in this world that we know now. If he has become mature in his spirit and he gives his spirit in obedience to what is correct, proper, right, and just, that is what we want. We all are trying to get there. Jesus Christ is a word and spirit from his Lord. So he typifies or represents in his type of man the spiritual life and how the spiritual life has to be disciplined, stand up to tests, because the world will try to take you out of that spirit. The Satan will come at you, himself, as it is written in the scripture about Jesus Christ.

Why thirty sections of Qur'an?

Why now do we have thirty sections for the Qur'an? This Qur'an is a book that if we follow it, it will take us to or develop us into that spiritual model that G_d wants for mankind. It will eventually develop you into that spiritual model that G_d wants to be leader for mankind, all people. Jesus Christ was betrayed, as I said, for 30 pieces of silver. It means they sold his worth as a leader leading people to give their life, their spirit into G_d's charge as servants of His for puritanism. They sold his worth for 30 pieces of silver and they got a puritanical society.

Created puritanical order

They sold his effort to bring the people into the spirit of obedience to G_d to bring about a puritanical society. They created a puritanical order to enforce purity on the people. They didn't have Jesus Christ's faith in people, so they enforced the law and that is what he came to break. He came to bring people out from under the law so that they would trust their own good nature and connect with G_d so that good nature would get its proper support and nourishment.

If you study the history of the Church that is exactly what happened. After Jesus Christ went away they became puritanical, puritans. They were hiding their human weaknesses. They weren't angels. They weren't protected or safe from error, morally, sexually, or whatever. But they hid it all. They would not let the public know that they were falling victim to these laws that they were enforcing upon people. So if you couldn't stand up under the law you were treated like an animal. You were not respected as a human being. They would beat you like an animal; holler at you like you were an animal; kill you as though you were an animal. You would not have to be a police officer to kill somebody. Any man of standing in their eyes could kill one of the common people and would not go to jail or anything. Believe me, it is almost like that in some countries right now, for common citizens. I can be a police officer and kill you and someone could say, "What happened?" The response would be, "Oh, this loud mouth, trouble maker, resisted me and I had to kill him." They would take his body away and that would be all. That goes on in the world, right now. Don't think every country is like this country where you are protected by law.

Human spirit by nature hungry

Prophet Muhammed said, "Matters are judged by intentions." So actually Jesus Christ was governed by intent. He said, "Don't you see I have to be about my father's business?" So his intention was always to serve G_d, to do what G_d put him in the world for. If you keep the intent right, pure, it will become automatic obedience for you. When it becomes automatic obedience, now, you've come into the spirit to obey. Al-Islam is designed to do that. The Qur'an is our salvation. Al-Islam is designed to bring us into that obedience to G_d and to develop us to have pure intentions, all clean, innocent intentions. And if we have that then the human spirit is free, meaning you can give your spirit to whatever you want to give it to. But the human spirit is also by nature hungry for the best possible condition. It wants the best possible condition for itself.

G_d will come and speak to you

So people will choose a moral life because they know that enables them to have more comfort for their spirit. They can live with a more comfortable mind and spirit. If they choose to follow G_d's guidance and follow it very determined about that, if nothing else is more important to them than that, then eventually their spirit will be the spirit of G_d's guidance. If you follow something your spirit will become that. If you follow the rappers your spirit becomes the spirit of rap music. Whatever you give your spirit to, whatever you follow, that is what you become. You have to have the intent, first. You have to intend to be right. If you don't intend to be right, then anything can take your spirit, the rappers or whatever. You have to intend to be right even if you don't know G_d. Prophet Muhammed didn't know G_d. If you intend to be right and you're so set upon that, you won't take anything from the world to give that up. They can't pay you to give that up.

If your intention is to be right like Prophet Muhammed was and like other servants of G_d were, then that intent will eventually bring you to seek G_d. Your mind won't be satisfied with the world. Things in the world will disappoint you one behind the other and you will be lost for something to support your good nature and your good intent. You will be crying out to the void, to the darkness, for light and G_d will come in there and speak to you. G_d will guide you. That is what happened to Prophet Muhammed. That is what happened to those before him. G_d will speak to you and guide you. That is the way it happens when you don't have guidance. But now that we have guidance from men who experienced those things wouldn't we be fools to put aside that guidance and follow just our good intent? Now in that case G_d is not with us because you're asking Him to help you, personally, and He already helped everybody. You want personal help but you won't follow what He revealed to Prophet Muhammed. So He is not going to help you. You will never get help. You have to recognize the good that is already here and support yourself with that good that is already here and then G_d will give you additional support, too. This is the way of G_d.

Spiritual dimension never solely in our control

This is not a small thing we're talking about. The spiritual dimension is never solely in our control. Nobody can control the spiritual dimension, alone. You can only control it with G_d and when He begins to guide you by way of inspiration or intuition you can't say, "I'm going to use my intuition to figure this out." It does not work that way. It comes but you do not know when it is coming. You can just hunger for it. Jesus Christ said, "Knock. Don't be impatient. Knock and someone will answer. The door will be opened if you just continue to knock". Don't give up. Have faith and keep trying to receive help for your good intent in your mind. You want to develop your mind for a particular purpose. You want to serve a particular cause and you need more help. You need more light on the subject matter. Don't give up. He said keep knocking. You're knocking on the door for help. You want somebody to answer it. We do it with dua' (informal, personal prayer), with salat. We also do it with our conscious mind. We talk directly to G_d as though He is there before us like a person and eventually you'll get the answer, if you keep the purity of intention.

Spirit always a future thing

It is a future thing. The spirit is always a future thing. It still has somewhere to go after the world is made right, because you're going to die. If G_d made me to want to obey Him and serve Him forever, why did He make me like this if I can't do that? This is wrong for Him to make me like this if I can't do that. I don't want to serve Him ten more years, or twenty more years, or a thousand more years. I want to serve Him forever, so why can't I do that? The will is in me to serve Him forever. So why can't I do that? I can and you can, too. That is what faith is all about. It is about believing that there is something beyond this world that we know, now.

Something continuous for scripture

The Qur'an was put in thirty parts to let us know that this is the Word of G_d that Jesus represented. Jesus represents a spirit and a word from G_d. He is a word and a spirit from G_d. So the word is revelation, not flesh and it is in the Gospel. He said, "Do this in remembrance of me". He gave them unleavened bread. They ate the bread and he said, "This is my flesh."

We find that there is something continuous for scripture, for the Word of G_d; and that is the interest or the desire to have more knowledge until the knowledge satisfies the souls of the seekers. We have in the Old Testament the pleading of souls to know the face of G_d, to see His face, to know the face of G_d. And in the New Testament we have the Prophet, Jesus, peace be on him, teaching the people in a very, I would say, unusual way. He taught by parables, for example hints, according to the Gospel, as it is written now, which you know is different from what Muslims believe. The original was called the Injeel. However, I believe that what I'm about to say to you is original and in the Gospel. That is, I believe that it did come in the Injeel. This particular, or I should say, peculiar method of teaching is where students are told to not use their own reasoning, not to apply their own mind, exert the faculties of their intellect, strain or exert the faculties of their intellect to form what they would say; but to trust G_d upon faith. They were told that when they met the occasion they would be given the words that they should speak. So as I look at that I see it saying that he taught people to trust inspiration; that they would be inspired. The same Gospel says of him, "He shall come upon clouds"; and another, "He shall come in clouds", or, "with clouds". Another is, "As the lightning shineth from the East even unto the West so shall the coming of the son of man be".

Mary sticks grooves in ground

In the Qur'an we have his birth happening in a very unusual way, to put it lightly. First, his mother, peace be upon her, she didn't have to be provided for. Her needs didn't have to be provided for by Zacharias, peace be upon Zacharias. Secondly, she was assisted by G_d when she was in a desperate situation to provide for her child, her new baby, peace be upon him. And Allah says in the Qur'an that He told her to take a little stick and make grooves in the earth and water would go through the grooves to the tree; and the tree would drop to her its sweet dates. When she was asked about him (Jesus Christ) according to the scripture, she said, "Consult the child", or, she pointed to the child, peace be upon the Prophet. Also, in the Qur'an Allah says to us that he spoke while he was yet in the cradle. He said, according to the Gospel as it is now, "I must go away. For if I go not away the Comforter will not come unto you", or, "be sent to you". He also said, "I will send him", meaning the Comforter and that the Comforter, the Spirit of Truth, would lead the people into all truth. This is the Gospel as it is now, the present Gospel, not the Qur'an. We don't want to mix anything here.

Now we know that Muslims believe the Comforter, or the one to lead into all truth, would be Muhammed, the Prophet, peace and blessings be on him. But let's look at something here. The Bible says, that is, G_d says in the Bible and G_d says in the Qur'an to Muhammed and the worlds that Christ Jesus, the Prophet, is a sign, a word and a spirit from his Lord, from Allah. There are scholarly persons in Islam that have searched the language of the Gospel before it was translated into English and they say that the word, "Paraclete", in the Gospel, is the same as, "Ahmad", in the Qur'an.

Jesus and Muhammed together

Then there is a change in his mission and he sends his disciples out, according to the Gospel, on a mission to give the Gospel to everybody, to the whole world. Our Prophet, peace be on him, it is reported that he said, "The day will come when they will see the Prophet Jesus and myself together". Peace be upon the Prophets. Now you know the ready meaning that any one of us would get is that it appears to the Christian world that the Prophet, Jesus, the Prophet of G_d and Muhammed, the Prophet of G_d, are at odds with each other. So the obvious message in that to us is that one day they will see that the two are not at odds with each other.

Word in soul of man trying to light intellect

But how will they come to arrive at that conclusion? That's more important than that first level reading of what that is saying to us in the world. I strongly believe that what the Prophet is saying to us is told in scripture, but most of us can't see it and the world hasn't seen it; that is, that Jesus Christ depicts the word. He's a personification of the word. The word of G_d is the same yesterday as it is today and it will be the same tomorrow. We believe the Qur'an to be the word of G_d. And if Jesus came, firstly, addressing his own people, the Jewish people, but then later sent his disciples out on a mission to give this to all the world, then Jesus was not only a depiction of the word of G_d in Israel, but the Word of G_d in the earth to all people; and that had to be told. But Muhammed, the Prophet, peace be upon him, is described by 'Aisha, radhi Allahu anha, may G_d be pleased with her, as the Word in the world, living, demonstrating, communicating, teaching. Now can't you see the two coming together, one personifying something that is enshrouded in the time of Muhammed? How do they differ? They are alike and they're different. How do they differ? Jesus, the Prophet, peace be upon him, he represents the word in the soul of man trying to light the intellect of man and trying to be perceived by the intellect of man. That's an inherent urge that G_d has created us with. Jesus represents that and he says, "I go away. I have to go away; for if I don't go away the Comforter will not come unto you". That's the word in Muhammed. It's going to come in Muhammed. "If you continue to trust this automatic nature you will never trust the neighboring intellect. So I'm going to pull myself out of the world. I do this because that's the purpose for which I was sent into the world. If I do this not the Comforter will not be sent to you, or, will not come unto you".

Can't you see how they come together? The two come together in humanity and also come together in the bigger stage, or on the bigger stage, the stage of knowledge, the stage of true revealed knowledge, the Qur'an. Both of them were the word of

G_d but established or brought into the world by two different means, by two different facets or properties of human nature. But they agree and they are necessarily connected in man and also in scripture.

The big fish of the water

The scripture says, "As Jonah was in the whale three days so shall the son of man be in the heart of the earth three days". So, "In the heart of the earth", what is this saying? Jonah was in the belly of a whale. A whale is the biggest fish. He is the master of the water for the fish. He swallows the little ones up with no effort at all except to open up his mouth. The current that he creates just sends them all down his throat. He's the big fish of the water. "The heart of the earth", means desire for the earth. Now the earth has a good reading and bad reading, too, because Allah speaks of, "Those who cling heavily". They're heavily pulled down to the earth because of their love and greed or desire for the earthly things. They're pulled down. They're heavily drawn to the earth. The earth gives us our sustenance, food, clothing shelter, and many other things. So, "In the heart of the earth", means because of worldliness, worldly appetites, he will be confined, imprisoned, like Jonah was in the whale. Now wasn't that the same thing? Wasn't that material greed? But it was not material greed in the material world. But it was material greed in the spiritual world. The big fish there is a sign of great wealth. Great wealth is a big fish.

Secular world has been coming for long time

What does it mean when you say a man is a, "Big fish"? The big fish means the wealthy in the spiritual life. So Jonah was a captive of the wealthy world in the spiritual life, the wealthy people of the spiritual life. The predicament for the Word of G_d would be that it would be a captive of the people who were greedy for the material world. They're in the material life. They're in the social life. They're in the community life. But they're greedy, too. What are they greedy for? It says, "In the heart of the earth", meaning they're greedy for the sciences of the earth, not just the material. They're greedy for the sciences, because the sciences will put them in a better position than the man who just has the material wealth. The sciences will give them control over the ones with material wealth. The sciences will give them the material wealth and also control, dominance. So he'd be the victim of the secular world. Don't think the secular world just came about. It's been coming for a long time. He would be the captive of the secular world, the world that wants to reorder the world upon the exact sciences.

Cross a sign of the world

It says in another part of the Bible or Gospel, "If they say he's on a mountain top, if they say he's in the sacred chamber, don't believe it." It goes on to say, "As the light shineth out of the East even unto the West". In explanation it means that, really, he won't be in the heart of the earth. The world has not put him there. But what they will put there is what they have control over. They don't have control over the word of G_d! Allah has control over that. Now you'll think they put him in the heart of the earth is saying the same thing, meaning he would be a victim. The people of the ascetic life, that order of the Christians, weren't they the captors of the world of material sciences and government and everything, Rome and others? And it didn't just start with the cross being like it is given, a center. You see, here, the cross is a sign of the world, the earth, or the world. That's what it's a sign of and it's no new thing. That's the way the Qur'an traces the origin of the cross, back to Egypt and when Isis crossed Osiris' path she formed a cross in the sky. She formed a cross in the sky of herself, her path and Osiris' path. The path of the two formed a cross in the heavens and the Egyptians, you can go see it right now in their museum like I have seen.

Christ the second cycle

The same soul that gets us into Paradise situates us to have an honorable and most resourceful 'aql (brain, intellect). That's that Christ entity, the soul that has a natural disposition to worship its Lord, to obey its lord and to pass on to the 'aql the responsibility for education and advancement. Now, of Jesus Christ the Bible says he's the second Adam. If Adam is the potential in man and Jesus Christ is the second Adam, he is the second phase, or the second expression or cycle of this potential in man. I'd rather use cycle. Adam is the first cycle of this potential in man. Jesus, peace be upon him, if he's the second Adam. I understand that to mean he is the second cycle for that potential.

Prophet Muhammed saw them in the heavens in the Ascension. You see, all of this comes from the Qur'an and the Prophet. I'm not the author of any of this. The Prophet saw these other prophets, peace be upon them, in the heavens, ascending up a ladder or up a progression from Adam, the first, and then Christ Jesus and John, the Baptist, on the second level. Do you know that man originally thought that there were seven planets, not nine? He thought there were seven planets. You can still maybe find in science the evidence that man thought that there were eight planets. Now in the time of the Prophet he was referring to or addressing the idea of eight worlds circling our world, because he was the eighth one, ascending the ladder of the seven and then leading the seven in worship.

The second Adam

Now, Christ Jesus, peace be upon him, as the second Adam then, would be the second cycle for this potential. The first Adam, he was created from the earth. The second one is Jesus, if we accept Jesus as the second Adam. I'm not saying I'm putting a stamp of approval on this language. I'm using this language only for the sake of understanding, for the sake of knowing where things are coming from. We have to know where things are coming from. So Jesus Christ then, peace be on him, he would be the second Adam and his birth is of a woman; not of the earth, but of a woman. Allah says in the Qur'an that the creation, or the parable, which means also the creation of Jesus, is as the parable, or the creation of Adam. It says that, "He created Adam from dust". You know Adam was created from water. He was created from clay, etc. But in that reference it is dust. "And Adam was created from dust!" That's to help us understand the creation of Jesus Christ.

What is the "dust"? Dust is the breakdown of the language of matter, "Ayah". G_d created the world and the world is ayahs, signs. So when it becomes dust we can't read it. It lost its script. It has no pattern. It has no sign of its evolution that we can read. So when it becomes dust we can't read it. And the Bible says, "Sit down in the dust!" Then it shows Job in another place sitting down in the dust and he's trying to get the logic back! He has companions who have their own cocky opinions and they're trying to persuade him to, "Give up this urge in you to try to make sense out of your G_d and your relationship to him!" But Job is so patient. He says, "I know I can't articulate what I'm sensing in my soul. I know I can't communicate to your rational ears what I feel in the deep vestibules of my soul. But it's so convincing to me, though I can't communicate it, intelligently. It's so convincing to me that I'm forced to have patience and wait on the Lord".

The dust of ignorance

That's Job. Isn't it beautiful? That's Job sitting down in the dust, the dust of ignorance; the absence of any logic that will hold up, that will stand up. Dust won't stand up. It rides the wind. It's so light that it rides the wind. Heavier dust will settle down if the wind becomes still enough. Heavier dust will settle down on the surface, but the least thing will disturb it and put it in the air, again; meaning man, when he has no rational foundation, intelligence, is suspended in spirituality and that's where Job was.

Job was in spirituality. His friends, his companions were in materialism and they were telling him to, "Curse this idea that you have of G_d. Just accept material reality and die here so that you can live in our world!"

Now, his creation is like the creation of Adam and Adam was created from dust. So what does this dust represent? You know some translators of, "dukhaan", they don't say, "smoke". They say "dust". "And the creation was as dust, suspended and in commotion." When you look at air in the sunlight you can see particles of dust in the air. And they all seem to be in commotion, moving like smoke, having the kind of appearance that smoke has when you look at smoke and the particles in the smoke; because, really, what you see as smoke is really particles. Those are really particles and they're in commotion. The particles are in commotion.

Gnost means urge for perception in soul

So, the dust represents the first state of the intellect, or the gnost. "Gnost" is a play on soul, but it's the urge for perception in the soul, this gnost. It's addressing the soul as the beginning, the womb, or the beginning place for the urge for perception in the intellect. The dust then is the gnostic state and G_d created Adam from dust. Now, we know He created Prophet Jesus, peace be upon him, from a womb; not from dust, but from a woman. Now, of Jesus it says that he was really before Adam though his genealogy is reasoned from Adam. He was in the mystical sense even before Adam. Now here is Jesus being born of a woman and Allah calls his conception and his birth, his creation, not a conception like we understand; but a creation like the creation of Adam. And he spoke while he was yet in the cradle. What does that tell us? It tells us that the process from mute expression to clear expression had started already when he was an infant in the cradle.

Three veils of darkness

Now don't forget. He's a sign of the word. But he's also a sign of the word in us! That's why it says, "I in G_d. I in you and you in me." So whatever he is that is in us and for him as a word, he's above us. He's in the heavens. But for the same thing in us, it's in the earth. Jesus existed in the womb of Mary and then he was given to the world from the womb of Mary. Speaking in the cradle is after he's separated from the womb of Mary. In the womb of Mary he was shrouded in three veils of darkness according to the Qur'an. It didn't say there was any exception. Every life that comes through the womb of a woman has to come through three veils of darkness. "Thulaathin" is the term in the Qur'an; thulaathin, from three, three veils of darkness.

Mary symbolic of best community

Now, what was his state in the womb? Dust. In the womb he was taken in as dust, with the water so it would be easy on the womb. In the womb he was taken in as dust and he was Adam in Mary, first, before he was Jesus. But under the process that fashioned him in the womb he is taken from dust and he beomes, 'alan nutfa, mudgha, idhama, lahma; then another creation; then the second Adam. So when he was born from the womb of Mary, who was symbolic of the best community, the best womb, the most lofty or highest raised up woman, now he's Jesus. Jesus was formed of Adam and became Jesus in the womb and then was delivered out to Mary as Jesus, the baby Jesus, peace be upon him. He is not directly the creation from dust. No, there were stages between dust and him. And also for Adam, there are stages between the dust form of Adam and the completed Adam. But when the completed Adam came into existence he was the product of dust; whereas, with Jesus he was not the product of dust. Dust came into the womb and the environment that evolved that dust made him the product of G_d. Adam was the product of G_d, too, but from dust. And here was Jesus, the product of

G_d, too, but not from dust; because in the womb the dust became Jesus, the baby, the life in the womb of his mother.

What is this talking about? This is talking about man arriving at conception or perception; the correct conception of things; the straining in the intelligence or in the intellect to perceive the right concept, having the right perception. This straining for Adam began in the dust state of his intellect.

A perfect learning environment

But for Christ Jesus, Mary's womb provided an environment for the dust that saved Jesus from having to come from the dust state. Her womb produced life and evolution for the dust that before he was formed, Jesus in the womb, the dust had already evolved to a state that represents a second progression for him. So that's the learning environment. There was a learning environment for Jesus Christ, peace be upon him, more than dust. There was a learning environment for him more than just dust.

Mary represents a wonderful learning environment. And what was her learning environment? "Do not hesitate to obey G_d! Hear and obey". Whenever there was a need for her to assist her son, the word, she had no question. She automatically, instantly, just did it. And when she was in doubt she was mute. She refused to speak. She pointed to the baby. Perfect obedience was the womb that produced him. Perfect obedience! "This new child here, you're his mother. Tell us something about Him". She pointed to the baby because she couldn't explain. She couldn't explain and the child was blessed to speak while yet in the cradle. So in the cradle he spoke to them.

Now, Jesus Christ, reportedly, is her son. We know it is her son, so to speak, because the Qur'an accepts that language, "The son of Mary". But, "The creation of G_d", is even more revealing for our understanding or for our need for understanding in our minds. So when he needed something she readily moved to do it. She got the vessels and she put them in the order that they were supposed to be in and everything. And she filled them with the water. She got the vessels and she filled them with water. Do you see, now, the water coming from the tree? She got the vessels and she filled them with water. This should be seen in the same kind of context or language environment. Nobody had to tell her how to do that. She did that on her own, just like a woman knows how to arrange for the guests that come to her house. She knows to get the tea pot and the tea cups and all that and to put them in the right traditional way; and when the time comes for you to drink she knows to pour the tea. She knows exactly when to pour the tea. She gets the signal from you. She gets the signal from the guests, from the husbandman, or from the boss of the house. She reads him and gets the signal that, "Now it's time for me to fill the cups". So she fills the cups.

Trees in the word of G_d

This is saying that she was perfectly obedient to the word of G_d, to the will of G_d, first. But after the word of G_d manifested then she was obedient to the word of G_d; perfectly obedient to Him, as the perfect wife, as a perfect mother. She didn't have a husband, so as a perfect mother. She's perfectly obedient, doing it without any hesitation; just automatically. So that was the environment that produced Jesus. But his creation is the same as Adam's. G_d produced Adam from a natural environment and the world was perhaps looking just like it looks now, except for these houses and everything. But as far as its natural make-up the earth probably had trees, animals and life abundantly, which it did. In the Garden we know that was the man. So He had to put him in the Garden. He made him and put him in the Garden. So, what is it saying? These trees don't represent trees in botany, the system of knowledge for plants. They don't represent trees in botany. They represent trees in the word of G_d. So when Adam came upon the earth, when Adam was created upon the earth from dust, he saw little trees.

So, for this Adam that G_d created from dust, in the context for Adam, the meaning for Adam, Adam was on the earth and there was nothing but dust. The whole earth was barren. He didn't see the trees, although they were there. He didn't see the animals, although they were there. And believe me if you don't have science you don't see them either, although they're there. You see them with your eyes, your eyes of flesh. You don't see them with the inner eye, the real eye, the eye of the intellect. You don't see them. You only see them with the eye of the intellect when you view them in the context of botany. Is that not true? Yes, when you view them in the context of botany then you see them in their reality. You see them as they really are. That's why it says, "This whole world, as we see it, is only "ghuruur". Who understands what "ghuruur" means in English?   It means, "Deception, illusion". Now, we know that that tree is not an illusion. I've touched it. I probably climbed it when I was a boy. "That tree's been in my yard for fifteen years. Don't tell me that's an illusion!" But in the higher language of knowledge it is an illusion, because you see it only as a physical object. When you see it in its evolution, its science, it's a language. It's an ayah (sign) from G_d. Even on a higher level it becomes a sign from G_d; a communication directly from G_d to man's soul and intellect; not only to to his intellect, to his soul, first, and then the intellect.

Environment as dust

So the environment then that made possible the creation or the womb, the environment as a womb for Adam, the first man, it was as dust. And G_d had to evolve his mental and intellectual perception, expand his vision, and nurture him until he came to the fruition, mental and intellectual fruition that would transform, completely, how he perceived things. Suddenly his environment of dust became a Garden of Paradise. Do you follow that? Now, Jesus Christ, peace be on him, his environment was the womb of Mary. We all will agree that if G_d created Adam or human beings on this earth, Mary was in the genealogy. She biologically came from Adam. So she definitely is the creation of G_d without any discussion, without the need for any discussion. But now what about him? He's mystified so we have to strain to understand his reality, or his birth, the reality of his coming into the world. But we know exactly how his mother got here. Just as all flesh got here, that's how his mother got here. Now we know that though she was born of human parents, a mother and a father, G_d's intervention was there.

Even when she was being conceived in her mother, G_d's intervention was there. When she was produced outside of the womb of her mother G_d's intervention was there. It was G_d all the time taking care of her needs directly, not through parents. So, really her son's birth is similar to her own. But only she has a father and mother, meaning that her understanding, her knowledge, came to her the same way that we understand that knowledge comes. But now knowledge is going to come to her son in an unusual way. In a very unusual way he's going to get knowledge. It's not going to come the way that we ordinarily understand that it comes.

"Who do you say I, the son of man am?"

He's going to be a prophet of G_d. But really her conditioning is the condition necessary for him to have the womb for his generation. He's being generated. When he comes out he is the product not of dust directly, only through Adam; only by the reasoning of his genealogy back to Adam. But he is the creation of G_d from Mary; not from dust, from Mary. He created Adam from dust and Jesus, too, from dust by reasoning of his genealogy back to Adam. But actually, he was created from Mary. And G_d says, "When He wills a thing it is only for him to say, 'Be!' and it is! Kun! Fiyakuun!" This is of Jesus' birth, how his creation is like that of Adam and when G_d wills a thing it's His to only say, "Be!" and it is! So Adam now was nothing but dust! And Allah said, "Be!" and it was; and it came to be.

Now Jesus was non-existing but G_d said to Mary's womb, "Be!" and it was. It came to be.

He is the son of man and in Christian language, the son of G_d. He's the son of man and he's the son of G_d. He on the one side is the son of Adam. Not an immediate father, but according to the genealogy, he's the son of Adam. Now, the Qur'an is easy on man. The Qur'an didn't want to say, "Your own New Testament says he is, "The son of Adam". What was Jesus Christ but a man? And he never wanted anybody to think he wasn't the son of man. He asked Peter, "Who do you say I, the son of man, am? Now in my reality, or in my common communication, you know I'm the son of man. But who am I on the higher reading?" "Oh Lord!" Peter said, "Son of the living G_d, because you're not flesh in the higher reading, you're revelation! You're the word of G_d! And man didn't produce that! G_d produced it. The word came from G_d!" But it's wrong even for us to say the Qur'an is the son of G_d, unless we have the son as sun. And it's not then the sun of G_d, because that kind of language will make us think that that is G_d's manifestation; that that is His embodiment; that the light that we see as revelation is Him in His Reality. That would be far from the truth! It is a manifestation of His Reality, a sign of His Reality, but not yet His Reality. No creature or creation can perceive His Reality without a reference, without a sign.

A potent germ in the social potential

Again, it says, "If they say, 'He's in the mountain', believe it not. If they say, 'He's in the sacred chambers', believe it not. But as Jonah was in the belly of the fish three days and three nights (meaning three veils of darkness) so shall the son of man be in the heart of the earth", the social potential. Heart of the earth means the social potential. He shall be in the social potential. He shall be a germ, a potent germ, in the social potential. He will be dormant in the body of mankind. But when the right thing happens in the environment, that dormant life shall become restless. It's going to be bored with its state. It's going to become active and it's going to rise up from the heart of the earth. A picture of that is practically every prophet, but we're going to look at Muhammed, the Prophet, peace be upon him.

The social potential in Muhammed was oppressed. His environment oppressed his social potential and it got so painful to him that he had to leave his environment and go to the cave, in seclusion, and strain to get revelation or some kind of help from whatever G_d was responsible for his being and the creation. And in time he was pressed three times; fee thulithan, three veils of darkness. He was pressed three times. The third time he received the light, communication. He began to read the revelation.

The word in Muhammed

So where was he before he received revelation? Before he began to be revealed to where was he? Understand that he was the word, too, living, demonstrating, communicating clearly and rationally to us in the world. He's not the word communicating by signs, like Jesus. He's the word communicating with clear, rational language in the world. He's the second promise of Jesus. He's the second Jesus.

Now, don't go and tell somebody that the Imam said Muhammed is Jesus. You'll be lying and you'll be wrong. I didn't say he was Jesus. I'm talking in the language of signs, fulfilling signs and I distinguish between him and Jesus. I just said that Jesus was the word communicating to us by signs and Muhammed is the word communicating to us with clear, rational language. So the second coming of Jesus is not the return of that Jesus. That's why it says, "I go away and you see me no more! The real me, this me that you identify, it's never coming back, again. But the same that produced me is going to happen again and nevertheless, you shall see me. Not this one, but you'll see the word in Muhammed!"

G_d's plan only for ideal human being

The Bible speaks of Jesus Christ as a word and it says he existed before the foundations of the world. That is to be understood in several ways. But one clear way is that G_d is saying that the world of mankind, the world we live in, it should conform to the plan of G_d and G_d's plan is for the ideal human being. It is not for every human being. It is only for the ideal human being. The ideal human being is man in his created excellence, the best moral life and the best rational life with all of the talents and possibilities for him in a real world. Jesus Christ is a sign of that and Muhammed, the Prophet, is the proof of that; not just a sign. Jesus Christ points to that in his creation. Muhammed is the fulfillment of that. It was achieved in the life of Muhammed, the Prophet; an excellent society, a just society, an enlightened society, a compassionate society, a humane society. All of that was achieved by Muhammed, the Prophet, in his lifetime. It is not something to point to. It is something that manifested under his leadership. It was produced by him leading the people to the way and as a result it fed the whole world, not just those immediate people. The language of Jesus Christ and Muhammed belong together. That is why Muhammed said in the end you shall see them together. Allah says in the Qur'an, "You will find the nearest people to you are those who call themselves, Nasara, the Christians", the people from Nazareth.

5

Muhammed: The Promised Human Destiny

Of the Prophet and his mission Allah says to us in the Qur'an that the purpose is to take us out of the darkness into the light. Of the light that G_d gives, divine light, G_d says of it, "It is light upon light". Most importantly then, we should see the city, the Promised Land, as a fulfillment of G_d's promise to lead us into the light, into the light that will remove all doubts or the need for searching for the light and bring satisfaction to the soul.

Prophet Muhammed said his mission would return to the people who supported his work. We know his companions were all with him but they did not know. None of them knew. G_d did not reveal to any of them, except Muhammed. So they were new and hearing everything for the first time. Abu Bakr and the rest of them, may G_d be pleased with them, they all were just like the most distant people from the Prophet in terms of their knowledge. They were hearing it for the first time, too. And some of them were opposed to it without knowledge. Umar, he was ready to even beat up the followers for listening to the Prophet and he came looking for his sister to give her a whipping for joining Muhammed, or listening to him. The Qur'an was being recited and he was hearing it. He got touched by it and he changed his mind. It turned him around. What he heard turned him around. One thing is sure. He spoke Arabic and he heard it in Arabic, in his own language and he knew that was something above their ability; that the Arabs had no ability to get that. So he was converted, but he had to be taught. He was in something totally and entirely new to him. That was all of them, Abu Bakr and all of them. That tells you something about the names they had. Abu Bakr means, father of a young camel. Muhammed, the Prophet was named Muhammed and Ahmad. He was called both and his name we understand. But the scholars know it has great significance in previous scripture. Would he have companions so close to him and their names have no meaning, no significance?

G_d's gift to you

Names have significance. Again, Abu Bakr means father of a young camel. It is one who protects and cares for something. So he is protecting and caring for a young camel. What is that young camel? The dawning of light and understanding in the intellect while it has not yet begun to read. It is intuitive. That is the camel. A camel finds the water. He does not have to see it. By instinct he finds it.

Abu Bakr as-Siddeeq means, the truthful one. So what is that saying? That says when Allah blesses you with the spirit of understanding, to seek understanding and the intuitive light bursts forth, you cannot lie. If it is ordinary human intuition, yes, that will not change you from a liar, not necessarily. But if Allah caused the dawning of light in you, that intuitive spark is G_d's gift to you and you cannot lie. The Qur'an says they both went as two arrows for the same target and they did not separate. They went right together, accompanied by the spirit of G_d. The spirit of man is accompanied by the spirit of G_d and they are going for the target to achieve what G_d wants man to achieve and they cannot lie. It is impossible for man to lie because he is going parallel with G_d, in perfect agreement with G_d. You see willingly or unwillingly and what we see happens in ordinary situations. But in this extraordinary situation where G_d Himself is present with the subject and He has given the subject of His Own Spirit and Will, that is different, much different. It is not a question of obeying or disobeying. There is no question.

The angel pressed Mohammed, the Prophet, peace be on him, three times before he could speak, before he could recite Qur'an. And we find another figure in the Bible who had lost his mission, Jonah, and G_d's books, the Qur'an and the Bible, seem to be giving us the same report on him, on his situation. The Bible says that after he went through his ordeal and was cast upon the bank of the river by the whale (big fish) he said, "I have a three day's journey". This is the Bible. "I have a three day's journey". In Qur'an he's shown as a figure that had been saved from one predicament but was in another. He was on the bank with the sun punishing his head and Allah's mercy caused a gourd plant, a vine plant like squash and other things, to grow up upon him, to climb upon him and put leaves above his head to protect his head from the sun. He said, "I have a three days journey," meaning he was not yet where he should be. "I have a three days journey".

Road to the Promised Land

Of the Prophet and his mission Allah says to us in the Qur'an that the purpose is to take us out of the darkness into the light. Of the light that G_d gives, divine light, G_d says of it, "It is light upon light". Most importantly then, we should see the city, the Promised Land, as a fulfillment of G_d's promise to lead us into the light, into the light that will remove all doubts or the need for searching for the light and bring satisfaction to the soul. Incidentally, or maybe not incidentally, the city of the Prophet is called, the City of the Light. Some seem to be very hesitant in embracing my interpretation of that progression, wa teeni (by the fig), wa zaytuun (by the olive), wa turi seeneen (by Mt. Sinai), wa hadhaal baladil amen (and this city of security); because on many occasions I have said that baladil ameen is the city of the Prophet (Madinah). It's not Mecca.

The road to the Promised Land begins where we originally were and man in his original place is told, symbolically, by the Ka'bah and the black stone in sacred, venerable Mecca. So then the journey should be from the Ka'bah to the light, to Madinah al-Munarrawah (the city of enlightenment); Light upon light.

The pure sciences bring them to dismiss G_d

Before continuing this I want to emphasize the caution that G_d gives about not wanting to get too close to the light with our eyes because it may blind us. The world's light is the darkness (dhulumaat) and the same steps followed by the humble servants of G_d that takes them into the nur (light) takes the world into the darkness. And their darkness is darkness upon darkness arising from the depths of the sea. So, they too, I repeat, follow the same procedure, i.e., teen (fig), zaytuun (olive). But their turi seeneen (Mt. Sinai) is not the turi seeneen of Moses. It's their faith in their own spirit and intuition, human intuition, not divinely sparked intuition. The end of their journey is what they call the pure sciences. But the pure sciences bring them to dismiss G_d. "G_d causes a problem, so dismiss G_d, be objective. You should obey matter, completely. As you should obey G_d obey matter. Only speak what matter says. Only report what matter says. Only come to the conclusions that matter implies or directs you to". Empiricism, I think they call it and that's what has given us the secular world that we have on us right now. That's their Madinah, their Madinah of darkness.

They say that in education there is teen, fig. You must use your imagination. You must trust creative thought. You must trust spontaneous bursts of energy in the intellect. They may even play some music for you while you're straining your brain, to help that happen. And they also say that they come up with one knowledge.

But out of the zaytuun (olive), or in the zaytuun, I should say, we read oneness. We read singleness. We read tauheed. We read Islamic monotheism, for want of a better expression. But for the secular world the zaytuun is science, one science; all sciences agreeing in one science, material science. Their turi seeneen is the intuitive edge. It is not the intuition that G_d gave the prophets, but the intuitive edge. Now where's the support for this kind of reasoning? Allah says in our holy book, the Qur'an, there were some who sought a hearing on high and Allah said, "You cannot and you will find that there will be shooting balls of fire and you cannot get there, illa bisultanin atheem, except as a big, mighty sultan (authority)". But He didn't say you couldn't get there.

Land of darkness

The jinn, a company of them, heard the recital of the Qur'an and they said, "We bear witness that this is a wonderful recital. None but G_d has done this". They were not inspired or given inspiration, their intuitive light in the intellect turned on, sparked, by divine gift or divine intervention. It's a property that they have. So just like we have in common with the jinn community the property of reasoning, we also have with them in common the property of intuitive insight. So they have their teen, their zaytun, and their turi see something. I can't say it's the turi seeneen. It's not Mt. Sinai. It's certainly not Mt. Sinai. But they have their turi see something and they want the baladil ameen, the society established upon trust, the society secured upon trust. They want that and not even America has it. Our society is a society under fear, not secured upon trust; and our society gives its citizens secular knowledge to support them and to guide them, not revelation. So even America's Promised Land is a land of darkness. Now going back to the zaytuun (olive) as a symbol, I said the zaytuun is to be understood as a symbol or signal to signal us to the idea of tauheed, oneness. But it is oneness in knowledge, in science; that one G_d did it all. Not an accident, not the Big Bang, but purpose, divine purpose, explains why this earth and this creation, this universe, is here bearing one design; the universal system of law, or laws.

Separation of knowledge

Before us the Jews claimed the olive. They still do. They are a people of the olive, the blessed olive and we know that we are closer to Christians in our spirit, but definitely close to the Jews in the reading of the concept of G_d (oneness); a blessed tree, an olive. For us science is not separated, just like life is not separated. For the western world, for America, Western Democracy, there's a separation of religion and government, or church and state as they put it. And you know for us there is no such separation. For Muslims there is no such separation. Also, for the West there's a separation of knowledge, pure truth, exactness, in the perception of knowledge, or pure knowledge or truth. But for us there is no separation. For them there is the world of physical science, the world of secularism, and the world of religious science, or spiritual science.

Now we know in Islam we have the branch called spiritual sciences from the "ruh", meaning spirit. But those sciences in our religion are not completely foreign to all the other sciences and that's what tauheed means, that there is oneness. There's oneness of knowledge and all knowledge belongs to that wholeness of knowledge. So there's seventy hundred or seventy thousand or whatever we might say, branches of spiritual science that have to be seen in connection with social science and all other sciences.

Again, we look at the Bible. The word of G_d, personified as Christ Jesus, peace be upon him, comes into the world not of water only, but of water and blood. So the water of science, or the science formed of water is in the heavens. "And the heavens and the earth were separated and the heavens was confused as churning smoke; and Allah directed Himself to the heavens and He said to the heavens and to the earth, 'Come ye together willingly or unwillingly'." And Allah, highly glorified is He, also said, "Can't you see that this creation was once one continuous whole?" It wasn't always just smoky heaven and an earth needing to be reconciled with a heaven that was in a bad shape.

Obedience to the Creator of matter

Our knowledge then is one. Creation is one. Knowledge is one. It is expressed in so many different forms but it is one. It is light upon light; light of a blessed tree, an olive. Its oil appears to be lit before there is fire. It gives off a light before there is fire. And the fire does not touch it. Doesn't this sound like empiricism, objectivity, where you're not forming anything until the essence tells you to form it and you're not forming it in any way that the essence is not saying for it? You see, our discipline is the same. Our discipline and our knowledge is the same as the jinn's discipline and his knowledge. But our result is different. His result is different. His obedience is to matter. Our obedience is to the Creator of the matter.

Prophets as single and plural figures

In the Qur'an and also in previous scriptures Adam, Abraham, Jesus Christ and other prophetic figures or prophets, servants of

G_d, are to be seen as single but also as plural figures. That means they do not only represent themselves, individually. Each of these great prophets I did not name them all. I just named a few of them, the main ones. All of these prophets they are special types of what G_d wants us to become ourselves. We should have their character. Our character should be growing more like the character of Muhammed, the Prophet. Our choices that we make in life should be guided by the principles that Muhammed, the Prophet, stood upon. So our choices will be good, right and will be the best choices. We should follow him in his excellence, generally speaking.

Muhammed the complete and perfect man

Allah is the Foreseer, the All Knowing and He has a plan to override all plans that may develop. His plan as I understand it, as I perceive it, was to bring more attention to this term, "khalifah," because the people were not educated enough back then to understand the term. They were just introduced to it. But the full meaning of it had not been given to them. It took them years of study, studying the life of the Prophet, and only a few of them, a select few among the top scientists or the top scholars of Islamic scientists, came to the conclusion that the Prophet is, "Rajilun ta'amun"; meaning that he is the perfect man. And he is also "Rajilun kamilun," the complete man. He is the complete man, and the complete man is the perfect man. Once G_d has completed the man as He intended for him to be made on this earth, then he becomes the perfect man. Perfect means meeting and satisfying the purpose, the desire, the intent, or whatever. That is perfect. So when the man has met the qualifications that were expected from him by G_d, then he is not only complete. He is also perfect.

"I shall be what I am"

The indication that Muhammed was perfect was with the proclaiming of the Qur'an to be complete and perfect. "On this day I have revealed for you your religion, completed My favor on you. I have perfected for you your religion, and completed My favor on you." So this is both. He completed His favor on us and perfected it. Completion and perfection go together. The completion is the perfection. When it is complete as G_d intended, it is the perfection. So Muhammed, according to Lady Aisha, was the reflection of the Qur'an. More so than that, he was the living Qur'an walking among us. That's how she described him. That's how the wife described the husband. So if he is, if he has been the vessel for the last revelation of the Qur'an and G_d has deposited the whole revelation into that vessel, it has caused the scholarly lady, Aisha, may G_d be pleased with her, to identify him as the embodiment of the Qur'an. That's what she said. You see, they didn't speak English. They spoke Arabic. He is the embodiment of the Qur'an. His identity then is really the embodiment of the Qur'an, the Qur'an walking, living among us expressing itself among us in marvelous words and also with deeds. If he was that and the Qur'an was completed and perfect, then he himself is also completed and perfect. The scholars reason then that Muhammed is the answer to an age long expectation that was on the wise of the world; that man was being moved by his Creator, by his Shaper, to better and more complete forms; that He is not finished. That's why it says, "I will be what I am. I shall be what I am. What I am I'm not yet. But I shall be what I am". So who could say that with any more confidence, comfort, than Adam, himself, if he knew his creation? Adam is the one who should say that. Adam represents the line of life that continues. So, if I were to say, "Muhammed was Adam", would I be incorrect? No, I would be perfectly correct. Muhammed was Adam in completion, in perfection. He is Adam.

Adam starts with the first creation, the first act of G_d to create His man. And mind you, Allah did not say to the angels, "I have created a man." G_d never said to the angels, "I have created a man. I want you to respect him." G_d said, "I am going

to create a man. I am going to create a khalifah." If you look at
the expression in the Qur'an and you, as a person who has
studied that word, its grammatical rules for it in grammar, how it
is to be explained, grammatically, you will know what G_d was
saying. He was saying, "Not that I created or that I am going to
create. By reasoning, yes, I am going to create". But actually
what G_d said is, "I am creating. I am in the act right now of
creating a khalifah. Anna Jaailun. I am making a creation.
Where am I making him, in heaven? No, I am making him, fil
ard, in the earth. I am making in the earth a khalifah". That is
what G_d says to the angels. But it's okay to translate it, "I am
going to make in the earth a khalifah." I'm not saying that we
should do away with that translation. But for teaching you should
make it clear that the verb says, "I am making. At this time I'm
doing this. I am making now. I am making a ruler, or a khalifah
in the earth."

G_d spoke to Adam. Adam was the first step in that work, in
that plan. Adam had in himself at that time, the concept G_d
created. And the concept at that time had all future possibilities
in it; although Adam at that time had not awakened to all of those
possibilities, all the future possibilities in him. Adam, when he
was made, he became father of all the generations, the father of
even our leader, our Prophet, the last Prophet, Muhammed.

Qur'an, the completion and perfection

We know according to the teachings of Prophet Muhammed,
Adam was the first concept, and out of him it was possible to
have all the other concepts. According to the teachings of the
Prophet, it was possible to have Jesus, the Christ, peace be upon
him; and it was possible to have after him, Joseph, Yusuf, peace
be upon him; and Idris, the fourth, peace be upon him; and
Harun, Aaron, the fifth, peace be upon him; and Musa, Moses,
the sixth, peace be upon him; and Ibraheem, Abraham, the
seventh, peace be upon him; and Muhammed, the completion of

all of them, who led them all in prayer, peace be upon him. He was the eighth and he led the seven in prayer.

This is Islamic teachings. He led the seven in prayer, even his father, Adam. He led his father, Adam, in prayer. He led his father Ibraheem, Abraham, in prayer. What is this telling us? It is telling us, "Here is the son, the last son in the prophetic progression. The last son, he leads even his two fathers in prayer". Did he lead them in anything else other than prayer? No, he only led them in prayer. What is the prayer? Prayer is the word. What is the word? The word is the Qur'an, the completion and the perfection that they all were aspiring to reach. Now here is the answer coming in the last one (Muhammed).

A far horizon

So he leads them in prayer to demonstrate to us by way of metaphor that here is the line of growth completed. Here is what Adam wanted. Here is what Christ Jesus wanted. Here is what Joseph wanted. Here is what Idris wanted. Here is what Aaron wanted. Here is what Moses wanted. Here is what Father Abraham wanted. This is what they all wanted. They wanted the arrow to reach its target. And here it is fired out of a bow, two traveling along to the destination as though they are one, reconciled perfectly; hitting the target perfectly. Qur'an says, "He met him on the far horizon". It was a long way from Adam's day, a far horizon. But that spirit finally got there and the job was complete and perfect. So this is the way we should understand it.

The knowledge we need

What is their justification for withholding this knowledge from their masses? They are slave masters. Intentionally, or unintentionally, they are slave masters. This is the common knowledge that will protect us and allow us to grow in strength, numbers and quality. This is the knowledge we need. If they

would give their following (I'm speaking of the Muslim world)
what I give they wouldn't have to worry about other religious
persons coming among them converting Muslims. There would
be no threat.

G_d has blessed us to come to Promised Land

How can there be a threat from a lower plane, to a higher
plane? G_d has been raising this up from lower planes to higher
planes and we claim that we sit with Abraham on the highest
plane. Then how can there be any threat to our zone from these
zones beneath us? This is not to show disrespect or to speak in a
disrespectful way of Christianity and Judaism. No, it is not that
at all. But it is simply to say that if that's all they have, what was
written for them, we don't have anything to worry about. Now
G_d has progressed their thinking, enabled them to extract from
what has been revealed to their prophets of old and to see the
light as it should be seen, in its completion and perfection. We
still don't have anything threatening from them. We should
make them our allies. We should become allies, because we
have been blessed by G_d, all of us, to come to the Promised
Land. Now, the purpose in me dwelling on the concept or the
idea of khalifah like this for all this time is because I believe that
is our strongest starting point when we want to understand what
is my existence? What is this thing here I call me, my flesh, my
body?

Little babies, they can teach us something. We say, "I'm
going to take a bath." But listen to the little baby, sometimes.
Sometimes there is a little alert baby in the house, or young child
in the house and you say, "Bath", and the baby will say, "Body.
"Do I have to wash my body?" Body, that's what you are. You
are a body and conscious. Conscious is in the body,
consciousness. We are talking about khalifah. We have dwelled
on this term all of this time to establish that the starting point for
us in understanding what we are and where we should be going
is khalifah. It gives us the complete picture that should be the

motivation in our life for every interest that we have. For every area or field of interest, khalifah should be the thing that generates confidence, hope in us. What can we not accomplish if we believe ourselves to be the khalifah, if we are believers in G_d?

Allah says that He has made everything in the sky. That means the universe, or the external world. He has made everything in the sky, the skies. He said skies, plural, "Sammawa", everything in the skies (and the world). The Qur'an says He made it to give its service to His khalifah. And He puts khalifah into the plural, meaning there will be khalifahs many all over the world and they will be generation after generation. They will continue just like the generation of man. In fact, the khalifah is the real line of the generations of man.

Khalifah the inheritance of the common person

He said that He has made us khulafah, or khalifahs in the earth. Then if we understand that we see that our starting point is khalifah, something that is not finished. The finish line for the khalifah is Muhammed and with him, all of us, if we follow his revelation, his pattern, his sewa and his uswaa. The starting point is that point. And as long as we perceive or see ourselves in our ability, in our creative ability, our inherent, creative ability, our native ability (all referring to the same thing) as khalifah, then we don't need anybody to motivate us. Who can motivate us better than G_d? Allah is the best to motivate us and Allah has said to us that all of us in our essence, all of us in our pristine nature, in our original capacity, have the potential to be His khalifah on this earth.

There are learned Muslims that I have met from different parts of the world, particularly from Pakistan and India, Palestinians, Saudis, Egyptians, etc., who have hinted very strongly to me that maybe Allah is making a khalifah in America. I have had some Asians come up to me and tell me this. I told them the same thing that I am telling you. The khalifah is not meant to be one man. We all are khalifah and if we have someone who qualifies to be the leader for us all, then, that person should simply be called a leader for that group, or the imam; but not khalifah. That term is reserved because it is the property of the common person. It is the inheritance of the common person. If you make it the title for your leader, you take the common peoples' mind off of it as their inheritance. They told me that and I witnessed inside that they were telling the truth. The khalifah is being made in America.

The light is called the life

The biggest job of light is conditioning the life. When light comes it doesn't only show you where you can go, but light makes you feel better inside. Light is relieving. Darkness is burdensome, especially when you want to do things. That's why G_d says He made the darkness to oppress and made the light to liberate. If light conditions us as well as clears the environment so we can see where to go and how to go about it, what is this conditioning? I was about to say the conditioning is that it makes you feel better and it makes you less burdened. It makes you more prepared to act or to move to do the things you have to do. It enlivens you. That's why the light is also called the life. It enlivens you. It makes you feel more alive, more active. You've got more energy to go now and it actually energizes you. Light energizes the spirit, just like the physical electricity energizes whatever it's sent into. The light energizes the spirit and it also comforts, gives comfort, because with light comes warmth, too.

The same light that gives us life, also gives us warmth; the sun, the original light; the biggest light we have; the one that only Allah hung up in the ceiling. When it is hung up there, all other lights lose their attention. They are not on stage anymore. They still exist, but they have no stage anymore once Allah hangs that big sun up there in the daytime. The sun, what is the role of that light? This is the light that we should be comparing the light of revelation with, sun and light. The sun and the light are signs, metaphors in our world, pointing us to, really, the true light, which is the light of revelation, the light of enlightenment, divine enlightenment. It is a sign of that. So let's look at the sun as a symbol now, as a sign of the real thing. This sun does not only clear the environment for us to see things and approach them more safely, and manage them more safely, etc. But it also energizes us. It contributes to a happier day for us. "Oh, look how bright it is. Isn't this a beautiful, bright day?"

The sun as symbol of happiness

I've heard men of wisdom in ancient scripture said that originally the sun was not a symbol of light, though it was the light. They said it was a symbol of happiness. The light, the sun, comes up, then happiness. The light of the sun meant happiness. The influence was happiness. So this is what it meant to ancient people, I am told and I believe it. I also did some research. I believe that in ancient times they saw it mainly as a symbol of happiness, not just light. So we know that it is the element behind all other developments. The sun influences weather more so than anything else. The sun acting upon the earth, acting upon the environment, maybe not directly all the time, but the sun in its role influences weather more than anything else. It is the force behind all weather cold, heat, rain, snow, sleet, everything; even tides. We say the moon controls the tides. That's what they say. The moon has no light of its own. The moon has no phases without the sun. Its phases are caused by the sun in its path and its relationship to the earth in their path around the sun. This is how we have to explain it. So to understand what happens to the moon, or what happens to the earth, we have to go to the sun to for an explanation.

Hamem masnun, warm soil

Now, plants grow not really because of rain. It is because of an additive. Plants grow because of the sun on the earth. The earth is the womb. The earth has the germ, but the sun must feed it. Now, before even there were germs in the earth, there was the sun and the sun in time made the germ for production. Scientific thinkers I am sure just instantly see it all, because we know before there was animal life there was plant life; then animal life, and a lot of dying and decaying finally made humus soil. That's how humus soil came into existence. From humus soil we get all the great productions, things coming up and dying. Death building up the soil is what has made it possible for us to have the richness of soil, humus that we have now.

G_d made His man from what? He made him from humus; not just soil; humus, "hamiem masnun". He made His man from hamiem masnun. He made His man from rich soil, fertile soil. And the expression, hamiem, is for the people of that time. In their language, hamiem means, "Warm". You get a lot of life and a lot of fertility in the soil and it's hotter than the soil without fertility. You who work with soil, you know. You put your hand in rich soil and feel it, then put it in sand. Sand is cooler. The more fertile soil is warmer. Masnun is a play on, "It might be offensive to your smell." So some translators say it's, "From stinky mud." They translate it, "From stinky mud". That's not an exact translation. That's not a perfect translation. There is nothing there that says, "Stinky". But it just says that it's warm. It has heat and it is something that you might despise. But out of that comes the possibilities for your life and your future.

So what built up all of that humus for the life to be created out of? The sun and the sun appeared to ancient man to rise up, really, from the bowels of the earth. You see, ancient man was not scientific, so he didn't know where the sun was coming up from. The only thing he saw was that it was coming up. When he was out at sea, it looked like it dripped some of its fire back into the water. So he thought it was coming out of the water. If he was at sea, or if he was on an ocean, then the ocean was the East. When it rolled out of the ocean he thought the sun was actually rising up out of the water. And it appears actually to be dropping some of its fire back into the water. I've seen it. It doesn't come up clean and clear. I mean clear of the water. When it rises up, you see beneath the sun the illusion that the sun looks like it's dripping some of its fire down into the water as it is coming up.

They took sun to be G_d

G_d has made the rising of the sun on ocean fronts, or lake fronts, or things like that, to appear to man as, actually, it is coming up out of the water. And if the land is open, it appears that it is coming up out of the earth, itself; that the sun is actually coming up out of the earth. If the land is not open like our city land, it looks like it is just flying across the sky. In any explanation, without science it is a spooky thing. Only science took the spook out of it. So we know now that it is just an inanimate body of fire, of burning material. We know that now, but ancient man did not. He was in the, "Thulamat", the oppressive darkness, and he was being formed. And G_d formed him to believe that a G_d is doing this and, "This is a sign to me that I have to read. So what, how shall I read this, my Lord?" He doesn't know his Lord. He doesn't know science, either. But he believes in his Lord. He knows that something did it all. "How am I to read this my Lord?" He finally comes to read it as G_d intended for him to read it. That's the potential of the sun rising up out of the earth. That's the potential of the sun coming up out of the earth to light the earth. Now look at your earth, your body. He also made a sun to rise in your body, in the dead matter of your body. And once your potential rises up and frees itself from the bowels of your earth, your personal body, it will light your world.

It was a sign that G_d gave ancient man.   And then the language becomes confused in time and they take the sun to be G_d.   I may say then that the khalifah can be metaphorically depicted as the sun, couldn't it?   We must come to understand religion, the life history of religion, because when we are talking about religion, today, we are talking about religion in a completely new picture, a new focus, or a view from that that men had before; what we call the traditional or classical prophets of G_d. You know, we talk about Adam. We have history. Man's history bears witness to certain developments in the life of religious people and we can go back to a time when religion for man was what the modern world came to call heathenism, paganism, or idol worship.

This is Muhammed's day

In this new world who is the leader? Muhammed, the Prophet, he is definitely the leader, the last, the seal of the prophets. Muhammed, the Prophet, this is his day; not 1000 years ago; not 1300 years ago. No, today is Muhammed ibn Abdullah's day and his day is the day that all the prophets wanted to see. All of the prophets were blessed with a help to bring them towards the day of Muhammed, the Prophet and the world is shaping, being shaped for Muhammed, for his leadership. Whether they know the Qur'an or are acquainted with the Qur'an, his sunnah, or not, they are going to be in the world of Muhammed and benefitting from the world of Muhammed. This is what I realize. I see and I know this. There is no guessing. I'm not confused. I'm not seeing this in part and I need something else to make it final. No, I'm seeing it in completion. I need nothing else. It is final. I don't lie to you. I'm a straight man. So this is what I see, Muhammed, the Prophet's day.

Discovering purity of human nature

I believe that our Prophet, Muhammed, peace be on him, was in a situation that didn't permit him to disclose what is the real, I would say, theme, overriding theme, for the Qur'an and for his own mission. It was because he was talking to persons who had been idol worshippers and a few who had been nature lovers; and those nature lovers were in his immediate circle. They were his companions. They're called in the Qur'an those who were upright in their nature. That's what the meaning is, those who were upright in their nature. Their name is in the Qur'an, the hunafaa. And when the Prophet got revelation and got connected with scripture he was told by G_d, by revelation, that Abraham was the first of the hunafaa, those upright in their nature. So what I have come to see and very clearly that hunafaa nature and the Prophet's main focus on humanity, helping humanity, is in the Bible. It's in the Gospel. It comes to light in the Gospel. And when he (Muhammed) said, "The world or the people will come to see myself and Christ together", I think that's what he was addressing; that he is all about uprightness, the inherent goodness in human nature that G_d put there.

I think when Christians say, "Christ within", they're saying the same thing Muslims are saying when they say, "The uswaa of Muhammed within", meaning his model, his human model. We're to emulate his human model. It's talking about discovering the purity of human nature that G_d put in us and living it to the best of our ability. Jesus Christ is put in the nativity scene with animals. So it's something he had in common, even with animals. That's what we're talking about, what G_d preserved in human beings, in nature and in creatures.

Muhammed comes in progression of revelation

Prophet Muhammed comes in the progression of the revelation. He comes in the sequence of prophets who came one after another, succeeding each other and the Qur'an is a book that is composed of books that came before. How wonderful Allah is. He has created man in the best of molds. Muhammed, the Prophet, the model man, was a fit person to lead people. Before G_d called him he was already fit in a world of ignorance, darkness, indecency, bestiality; a world of violence and the sacrifice of innocent lives. It was a world that allowed the murder of babies before they could even be taught how to live, especially the girls that they did not want.

In that time and in that kind of world a man was able to keep his best life that G_d created Adam with intact. Adam lost his best life to the subtle deceits of the Shaitan. As we know, he was deceived by the subtle words of the Shaitan to come out of the nature that G_d had put him in and made him for. Muhammed, the Prophet, had survived in a world of corruption, ignorance, violence and the loss of respect for human life. He survived in such a world, was not worshiping any idols and was not behaving in any way that G_d would not approve. So he was, again, like Ismail, the son of Abraham, a lamb without spot or blemish; like Christ Jesus and others who were also called by such wonderful descriptions, or given such wonderful descriptions. The leader in Islam, Muhammed, the Prophet, he established for us the ummah, the global community, the worldwide association or community of Muslims. He established that for us under G_d, following G_d's guidance and he established it after the order of Abraham.

Abraham was a community

Some time ago when I was visiting Saudi Arabia, a learned sheik told me, "Imam Mohammed, you know Abraham is a community", to tell me he's not just an individual figure. But he is a figure or type of a whole community. When we study Jesus Christ in the scriptures that were given to the people of the book and also in Islamic knowledge, we see Jesus Christ, also, as a mysterious sign of the community, the community of Adam, the community of mankind. We are after that order. Muhammed, the Prophet, taught us and we know Allah says to us in the Qur'an, "You will find the Christians, those who call themselves Nasara (the old name for the Christians, the people of Nazareth) to be the nearest to you"; that is, the nearest to you in the practice of religion. He also said that in the end the world, the world of the religious people, the people of the book and us, will see Muhammed, the Prophet, the last Prophet, and Jesus Christ, G_d's Prophet and messenger, also, together.

Qur'an G_d's last address

So let us keep our spirit correct by not seeing Islam in opposition to Christianity. Islam is in opposition to any untruth, any falsehood, or any indecency. Islam is in opposition to nothing but what Allah has ordered it to be in opposition to. Islam doesn't pick up any personal quarrel with anybody, any idea or anything. Our obedience is to our G_d, Who revealed scripture to the people before. He revealed the Qur'an as an explanation, a clear explanation on that that was revealed before. So we must understand from the words of G_d in the Qur'an that the Qur'an and Islam are G_d's last address regarding what He said to man, or what He has revealed to man. Our guidance is the Qur'an and we would hope that the whole world of religion would get acquainted with the Qur'an so they will know what G_d has said more recently on what is right and what is wrong, when it comes to what He said to mankind. He spoke to many prophets before. He spoke even to females, we are told, in the Qur'an. He spoke, lastly, to Muhammed, the model man that was prophesied to come.

Muhammed the last stone

It was prophesied that this day would come. Jesus Christ pointed to Muhammed. All the prophets pointed to Muhammed and that was told to us in the sign that's given to us in the Ascension (Miraj) and travels of Muhammed, the Night Visit of Muhammed, when he was seen leading the prophets in prayer. Here is revelation for the Muslims to tell us that Muhammed is the last one and the last one is completing what the previous ones were all about. Muhammed in speaking on or addressing this particular point that I'm making now, said that there was a house being built; and it was being built by the ones sent by G_d, the prophets, servants and messengers of G_d. But there was one stone left to be placed. It had not been placed to complete the structure of that house and he said he is that one. He is that last stone and we know that the last stone, it is the cornerstone. It's the stone that makes sense of the whole structure. The whole structure is left without sense until that stone is put there. That stone is the stone of universal brotherhood, the stone of universal truth and the stone of oneness for not only G_d, but oneness for mankind.

The time of conclusion

So, we're living in the time when things are being concluded for the human family on this earth. Questions that we couldn't answer before those questions are being addressed now and there is a determination in the highest minds, governments and religions to conclude the matter. We should have enough progress for our intelligence and our world to come to the conclusion that concludes these matters. So we are living in the time of conclusion. Things are going to be solved. Questions are going to be answered. Problems are going to be solved. The world is going to be a much better world and you're going to see Muhammed and Christ Jesus come together. As Prophet Muhammed said, "They shall see Christ Jesus and Muhammed together". You're going to see them come together very soon. In fact, they're coming together, already, Christ Jesus and Muhammed. And it can only happen in the conclusion of things or have expression in religion, theology, deep religious studies in ontology and eschatology that are seeking to perceive how things began and how things will end.

We are living in the time now when our great minds must see the signs all over the world. In every nation you can see it, that man has come to a state of mind and a state of reality that forces him to look back at his history and perceive how he has come from where he was in the beginning to where he is now; and then anticipate the conclusion of these things and turn to G_d before he gets to his answer. He will turn to G_d before he gets to his answer, why? It is because G_d has dominated the scene. If you can't see it, believe me, I see it.

Ocean symbolic of collective soul

In a strong hadith taken to be very authentic, Muhammed, the Prophet, said G_d offered him the way to carry out his mission through the mountains or through the plains and he chose to go through the plains. This tells us that he is one of those figures who levels the playing field, or levels the mountains. But then it was necessary, because G_d said if He had not placed mountains on the earth then the earth would have not been stable; and it would have brought down society's structures, or left man's world in ruins. That is what it means.

There is more than one picture of the mountains. Some mountains are high but have no snow. They are in hot regions, ascend very high and they are luxurious. They have an abundance of beauty and value exposed; whereas, some mountains, they are just rocky, stony. They are not supporting vegetation, life, whatever; and all of them as they ascend so high their tops are very cold. They ascend high enough no matter where it is. It could be in Africa, anywhere where the tops of the mountains are very cold. But look at the mercy. In it being cold like that the collected water turns to ice. They collect and store clean, good water and when they experience warm times the water melts and runs down the mountain and becomes rivers with a mission to relive misery in suffering society.

Where are the rivers headed?

John baptized people in the river and where are these rivers headed? They are headed for the ocean, the lowest spots on earth. So all that on high shall yield in time and let its purity go down to the lowest of the low and it's going to end up depositing itself in the ocean. The ocean is symbolic of the collective soul. The biggest body of water, the biggest spirituality that you can find is the ocean and what is that? It is man's common soul. That is where all people come together, all spiritual entities come together.

Indeed, the aim is for us to become oceanic, not little, small lakes and rivers. And the oceans do not exist without salt, right? Salt leaves a bad taste in your mouth. If you get too much, you want to rinse it out. When mankind comes together without discriminating against people because of race and national origin or anything, what are we doing? We're registering the burden on the human soul and we get a bit salty, don't we? We say we have to organize and change things. Allah loves that, too, in man's soul. That is why it says in the book (Qur'an) "From the sweet water and the salty water is delicious meat".

Meet in ocean of souls

So this language is so beautiful when we free ourselves. As long as we are in the prisons of our own narrow thinking we cannot see the full beauty of G_d's revelation. But if we meet in the ocean of the souls of mankind, we can see it there and those creatures there they move about in a serious fashion. You do not see fish and whatever in an ocean moving about like they are going to a carnival, to the playground or something. They move around like serious business, like they are seeking serious business. Those little playful fish, sweet water fish, they are just flipping around. However, in that big ocean the creatures are moving with cautious precision, the whales and the sharks, etc.

In the Qur'an the fish that Moses was searching for moved through the water straight as though in a channel. Some fish, for example salmon, when they go to spawn, they are headed in a definite direction and they continue in that direction until they get there. So what it is saying to us is that there must be a higher purpose in the intellect of man to keep, or to hold his intellectual vision so he does not lose it, or have things distract him from bringing unity to his life. Purpose brings unity to our life. When you give yourself to a higher purpose it serves to unify your intellect where your intellect is not going this way and that way and every way. So a definite aim or purpose serves the unity; or a better word in this expression would be integrity. It serves to bring about integrity for man when he has a higher purpose, wholeness of conscious, where his mind has something to protect and advance his vision going forward; and his thoughts for his vision advancing, forward and in harmony. So it serves to unify or bring about integrity for man's intellect and consciousness.

Intent in religion and scripture

Integrity means wholeness, but it also means, harmony, agreement, and a workable unity. That is very important for a reproductive mind. It has to achieve a higher purpose, something that appeals to the mind's need for peace, harmony and integrity. It means agreement in a definite focus. A person of integrity is a very strong person because something higher has formed, ordered, contributed to their mind coming to order and having a vision and a definite plan and a commitment to not violate the principle for the plan. Stay moral. Stay rational. Stay focused. Stay obedient to a higher cause. That is what makes great people. That is the intent in religion and scripture. It is not always respected in religion as expressed by preachers or leaders. But that is what scripture wants in man, to find the higher cause that can bring about the best order for his intellect, for his mind. It situates him as a thinker, or a visionary to accomplish all that G_d created man to accomplish on this planet, earth.

Heaven now and later

Also in the Bible it says, "No one has ascended to heaven who was not already in heaven". So even going to heaven must be experienced or realized on this earth, in these natural circumstances. And if you do not achieve it in these natural circumstances, you will never achieve it. That is the Bible. Man is deprived of his complete evolution, for lack of a better word right now. He is deprived of his complete vision and perception and is limited. He is held back from realizing his complete, his full possibility for perception, vision and understanding in this world. What holds him back is incorrect delivery of G_d's word. They do not deliver it correctly. So by not delivering it correctly it causes man to lose the way that G_d created for him.

Back to Eden

So then to bring him back he has to go back to the origin, or back to Eden. What is Eden? Eden is his first conception, or his first awareness of his existence as a thinking being in creation before man made anything. There was nothing man-made. There was nothing he could point to as his own work. That is going back in his thinking, to the origin. So that is what you have to do. You have to go back to the religion of origin, the origin upon which He structured man or fashioned mankind, society and everything, men and women, too.

But he is not able to go back without G_d's guidance. He cannot find his way and G_d's guidance is always close. In the Qur'an it says, "If my servant asks about Me, tell him I am near." As close as your creation, that is where His guidance is. Abraham said, "The one who created me shall guide me." Abraham also said, "All of these other gods are my enemies except the One Who is the Lord of all of the worlds". He's the One Who has evolved all mankind, not just one nation, one people, all of them; not only Israel, but all worlds.

Soul has the savior in it

But they mystify the power of our own souls to deliver us from the world's problems, free us from the world's problems. They mystify it so much that you think it is not possible for you, that you are hopeless. Christ is salvation, meaning that Christ is in you, your savior is in you. You are created with your savior inside of you. That is what Christ said, "I in the father, the father in me and I in you." And Muhammed said, "Say to them I am a mortal just like you." Whatever is in my soul is in your soul. That is what it means. Whatever is my true nature is your true nature.

This is a language of deliverance and salvation. And it can save us and any other people who are under the world's darkness. It can save all of us. But the mystifying does not help at all. When they arrested Jesus what did he say? "Why do you arrest me in the night when everything that I've done was in the day?" So the Qur'an comes. What is the Qur'an? It is the clear understanding for the clear report given. The Arabic word, "Mubeen," means, "Very clear, perfectly clear; openly expressed", not secretly expressed.

False religion persecutes scholars

Muhammed, the Prophet, wanted to see all of us reach that. When he said to his followers, "Meet me at the water pool," the language used is like a big bath tub. So that says that his mission was to bring us all together for a refreshing bath. In the Qur'an, it pictures him as the unlettered Prophet mentioned in the books that came before, really mentioned in the Torah and the Gospel. What is his mission? His mission is to purify you and to free you from every yoke and bond of slavery. All that enslaves the mind he came to free us from it. And a yoke is what they put on cows. So to take the yoke off of us means to free the intellect of the scholar, because false religion persecutes the scholars.

The philosopher (Socrates) was imprisoned and then they gave him hemlock to execute him, to kill him. It does not really mean they killed him, but they locked his "hem" that causes rigor mortis in his blood that feeds his brain and his whole body. That is hemlock. Hemoglobin has to do with the blood. A woman who was a sinner was laying on the ground. She didn't feel clean enough to even stand up before Jesus. She just stayed stretched out on the ground. She touched the hem of his garment and was healed. The hem of his garment forms a wide circle. But that wide circle is down there low at the feet with the common man. She touched it and was healed. She understood his social mission that it was for the common people. It came all the way down to her. A sinner was healed and as that song says, "How sweet it is!"

Muhammed established in history

All of this I'm saying to you to say that we're living in the conclusion of the great issues for man in scripture. He starts out innocent like a new baby from his mother that has not been influenced, has not been lead astray. He starts out innocent as though in a Garden of Paradise, an Eden of the Bible. He starts out in an innocent life in an environment that supports his innocent life developing and progressing. Accomplishments, especially for his comforts, began to take his focus away from obedience to consuming and creating comforts for himself. He falls victim to his need to have comforts or pleasures and the pleasure appetite eventually destroys him.

Prophet Muhammed is established in history and history says that he was established in the public of his time as the honest and trustworthy one. And he was also established as the truthful one. Now these two attributes of Muhammed, the Prophet, in Arabic, "Al Ameen, the trustworthy one" and "As Saadiq, the truthful one, these two words, I find in the Bible. They are in the major themes of the Bible that begin in Genesis and go to the end of the Bible, to the end of Revelations. These two names are in that great scheme, that great movement of scripture that takes us from the beginning of man's creation to where he should be in the end. According to our knowledge of al-Islam and according to my knowledge of the Bible, our world depends on us having leadership that is honest, trustworthy and truthful and we are given a lot of help.

There's room enough. The earth is real big. You are not going to lose anything. You'll gain more. They'll have a chance and by them being given more opportunity you will have more riches, although it doesn't say all that. Isn't that what happens? When a democratic order is established it gives more equal opportunities to the members of that society, especially in past times. It can happen now if these people do the right thing. In past times what happened was they had more men to produce. So production increased greatly and as a result of that the top percentage of the people became richer, more powerful.

A new order of mountains

Again, the mountain is a good descriptor. The mountain is wide in its base, but as you go up the mountain it gets smaller. That's the way society is. It's never going to change. It says the mountain is going be leveled, in principle. But, the mountain is going to stay and the same is true for society. It is the nature of society that only a few people can be at the top. A number of people are going to be in the middle and a great majority at the bottom. The wise know that the majority of people in society are always going to be at the bottom. That's the way it is. But those at the top should bring the utility down within their reach. So we shouldn't live in the top of the mountain. We should live on the plains and work to create the good life on the plains with the people. Then our institutions of learning will be up in the mountain. Our great sciences will be up in the mountains. But our livelihood will be down here on the plains with everybody else. The Qur'an says it beautifully. It says if Allah hadn't established mountains on earth, the earth would have given way with us.

So if you want the earth you had better keep the mountains. Mountains are going be made level only in principle and only as a consequence of their not accepting to abide by the principle of equality that G_d wants, justice and equality. Then, they will be leveled, meaning that all the high establishments will be brought down to the level of the common man. That's the defeat of all these kingdoms. When the right order comes isn't that what it does? The right order levels the mountain and makes all the established societies, or orders have to undo everything they did, give up what they have done and accept to start all over with the common man. So, all of these governments are going to be done away with. All the governments as you know them are going be done away with and everything will be reduced to the level of the common man.

That's what happens with enlightenment. All the great orders have to accept to come down to the level of the common man. They will have to give up their kingdoms and governments and accept to start all over again. It doesn't mean that the mountain is not going be raised up again. A new order of mountains is coming. That's why all of these have to be leveled. We will never have a situation where there are no mountains.

The higher existence Allah intends for all human beings

We have to be motivated and self-driven. The human being is not a donkey. The human being is not a cow. The human being is above all animals. The human appetite is not limited to physical appearance and physical concerns, or material interest and material concerns. Human life begins to show itself when man translates material things into higher concepts. When he translates those things that appear to be no more than physical things in the eyes of most he translates them in a way to present a higher reading, a higher script, a higher definition of those things. For the light of physical things is not as high as the light of intelligence and scientific insight. Scientific insight is a higher reading of what appears to be material and physical, only. So man, the human person, has been created for this much higher existence. And in all of us should be an appetite for the higher existence that Allah intends for all human beings.

Don't let the world dampen spirit

These people who are being formed in the hells of the street can't you see why they are not productive, why they cannot contribute to the establishment, to the structures in their neighborhoods? They offer nothing because they are created in hell. But, if we remain devoted to this religion we will create an excellent environment. We are being formed in heaven right now, those who are sensitive to what is happening. We are being formed in heaven right now and we can go in the world and be productive. They won't cripple us with their sins and our souls will be sensitive to the needs of human life. Each one will go his own way to his own interest. We all will contribute to the building of a new world and it is happening all the time. It is not to come.

So when we look at the objective world we see two worlds and not just one. Shouldn't we see our world, the world of the righteous trying to obey G_d and the world of those who don't care? Don't let the world of those who don't care dampen our spirit or hurt us in anyway. Strive to keep our own world in our eyes so our own world feeds our life. It says don't even gaze upon the wicked world, because if you turn your eyes and look at that focus you are going to be fed by the wrong thing. You will have the wrong spirits coming into your life. So keep your vision, eyes, focused on your life and your world and that will keep you strong to survive all of the harm from the things that are happening in the world of the ungodly. The devil is constantly trying to build the world of the ungodly so that it will choke out our life and we will have no place to live. But he is going to fail. He is failing and he is going to continue to fail.

A people no more

In the Qur'an a people are called by the Arabic term, "Qom". From the same root that means, "People", you also get the word, "Standing." So to be a people you have to have establishment.

The same word gives us the meaning, "Standing, establishment". So a people sitting idle are they really a people in the true meaning of scripture? No, they are not people. Those who are planning to undo everybody else, they will succeed and be the masters if they can, as the scripture says, "Cast our bands asunder". Asunder means to throw them off, like we are all together by a rope or a belt and they take it off of us, break the belt and throw it away. That is casting it asunder. It can't be of any use to us anymore and they throw it away. What kind of bands? Ties of parent and children, husband and wife, ties of human interest and community interest, if all these are cast asunder, you can't be a people anymore.

That is what has happened to most of the people of the world. Their language has been confounded and their bands have been cast asunder. They are not productive societies anymore. Look at how the world is all messed up. We think of just Africa, but Europe is dying, too. It is struggling for its life. Somebody set us up to see black and white and that is the way we were seeing things for a long time while they were working on us to make us non-productive.

One day a great new leadership

It only takes a few to wake up and save the future for the many. There are strong ones among the whites and strong ones among the blacks and others who are holding their life and waking up to just what is going on. In time we will have a great new leadership and we will recover. But in the meantime, the new reality, this new world situation we're in, demands that those who know don't just know for relief. Relief is to free you to have more energy, more faith to work. We should be working hard, giving all of our energy to work hard on the life we're building. Don't put all your energy outside of the work field. Know the field of work that we're in and work hard to build on our grounds, not spread it all out and go everywhere with it; and you just have a good feeling that, "My heart has been relieved. I think I understand this world". No, you are freed up to work more.

The vertical path, man's ascending upward, means it is the path of his excellence in his spiritual soul and spiritual body. The path of virtues, principles, righteousness, purity, innocence and justice, is the vertical path. We can only ascend along the path of our progress for our soul and intellect. We can only ascend so high and the burden is going to get too heavy on us from down here. The misery down below is going to bother you so much you're going to have to come down from heaven or down from the mountain and do your job. And it is not going to be easy. G_d says in the Qur'an, "Peace it is until the rise of the dawn or the spread of the dawn".

The greatest conquest

One religious thinker is reported to have said, "The conquest of the soul is the greatest conquest." What he means is bringing the soul to be in your control for the pleasure or the sake of G_d is the greatest conquest. Everything that is other than that we have to strive to manage it, to have it in our control. Allah has not given us a brain, intellect, spirituality, or a soul for us to follow it. No, we follow G_d's direction in it, but we are to be the masters of it. We are to bring it into our own control. Before we want to manage business or the world or other people we should try to manage the forces in our own creation.

Your sensuality, your desires for women, your hunger for money, your desire to be important or to have great stature, or a great place in the world, you have to manage that. If you can't manage your desires you're going to hell. There's only one way to go if you let your desires take over and you do not rule your desires without the guidance of G_d or at least with the guidance of your best intelligence and your best moral sense. If you do not let the guidance of God rule in your life you are going to hell; not tomorrow, but right now. Whoever gives up on that he goes into hell, immediately, while living in his body and hell will increase for him until he turns back from that or repents that behavior. You were created to be khalifah, meaning you were created to master your own self, to be the boss and the manager of your own forces in your life. All of our children should be told that and I guarantee we will have a much more powerful and intelligent generation.

The Promised Human Destiny

So we pray that Allah continues to aid us, forgive us our errors until we come to the bath hole of our Prophet Muhammed (the prayers and the peace be on him), the place of abundance, the abundance that Allah promises His Prophet. His Prophet said, peace be on him, to his disciples, "Meet me at the Bath Pool of Abundance". Now, he won't be there with us in the flesh. That's where G_d was directing him and he knew he was not to realize it in his individual, personal lifetime. But he was to realize it in his lifetime in the community and that one day he would come to that Fount of Abundance through our lives. And when we get there we'll know how we got there and we will greet our Prophet there, "As-Salaamu Alaikum, yaa Rasulullah (Peace be upon you, oh Messenger of G_d). We're indebted to the guidance of G_d and your tradition, your uswaa, for this meeting at the Fount of Abundance!"

The full fruition of the human potential, that's where we're headed, G_d willing. So we ask G_d to reward us to have children who will keep in this direction so that one day we will meet the Prophet, the prayers and the peace be on him, at the Bath Pool of Abundance, the Fountain of Abundance...the Promised Human Destiny.